The Bible offers practical help in

preparation for marriage success.

Where can you better learn of the

problems and possibilities of

marriage than from God, the first

Matchmaker? Each chapter of this

book is a biblical look at some

phase of marriage preparation—

a little advice before you marry.

BEFORE YOU MARRY

J. Allan Petersen

Living Books®
Tyndale House Publishers, Inc.
Wheaton, Illinois

CONTENTS

Cover illustration copyright © 1993 by Lori Osiecki.

Living Books is a registered trademark of Tyndale House Publishers, Inc.

First Living Book edition 1994

Library of Congress Catalog Card Number: 94-60616

ISBN: 8423-1221-8

Printed in the United States of America

00 99 98 97 96 95 94
8   7   6   5   4   3   2   1

PREFACE

*N*o sane person would ever leap blindfolded over a cliff with nothing but a hope that it would prove to be a good decision. No wise person would commit himself to live in a strange land without knowing something about what to expect and the difficulties he would inevitably face. No one foolishly commits himself to playing a game without knowledge of the rules that determine its success or failure.

Yet millions of young men and women take these same unbelievable risks when it comes to marriage. They feel their marriage will somehow be happier than most marriages they have observed. But they have no valid reason to expect it. Obviously, their relationship will certainly be better than their parents', though all they know is what their parents have told them. They are sure that marriage is a box full of goodies received with the license and ceremony and that it always remains full regardless of what is put in or taken out.

It is no surprise, then, that the highest incidence of divorce is found in the below twenty-five age group—three times that of the overall rate. Wives under twenty are involved in almost half of all divorces recorded yearly.

Clearly, more premarital counsel is needed. The Bible offers practical help in preparation for marriage success. Where can you better learn of the problems of possibilities in marriage than from God, the first Matchmaker? Each chapter of this study is a biblical look at some phase of marriage preparation—a little advice before you marry.

How to Get the Most from This Book

or the Lord gives wisdom, and from his mouth come knowledge and understanding" (Proverbs 2:6)

This series of studies has been designed to enable you to search the Scriptures and come up with answers to questions concerning dating, marriage, and the family. They should help you to acquire knowledge and understanding concerning these all-important subjects.

The first three chapters pertain primarily to preparation for marriage, while the following chapters deal more directly with marriage itself. This book is intended for use by the following:

1. *An individual,* who will find it helpful in developing sound attitudes toward the problems and potentials of dating relationships, as well as married life.

2. *An engaged couple* preparing for marriage, who can share their findings as they work through a chapter together. It may be preferable, however, because of

time pressures, for them to work through the material in each chapter individually, then set aside a time to share their answers, reactions, and applications gained from that particular chapter.

3. *A small group,* each person preparing the material in a chapter beforehand and then meeting to discuss it. Maximum benefit from *Before You Marry* is derived from the interaction that occurs in these small groups where people can learn from one another as they share their thinking and research.

4. *A Sunday school class* of single adults of college age and above who can complete the material in one thirteen-week Sunday school quarter by filling in the material weekly as homework. The Sunday school class could be led either by the regular teacher or divided into smaller interaction groups with a leader assigned to guide each one. Each person should have his own copy of *Before You Marry*.

If you are studying this alone, you will get maximum benefit if you have a Bible and pen beside you as you begin. Occasionally a dictionary will be needed. Each question will direct you to a passage of Scripture. After reading the passage, write the answer in your own words. References are given in this way: Ephesians 5:21. This means the book of Ephesians, chapter 5, verse 21.

Be sure to pray for understanding as you work through each chapter. It may help to set aside a regular time to work through the material, allowing yourself adequate time—one hour or so—to complete the material. Some chapters are longer than others. It may work best for you to take a few questions each day instead of trying to finish the material in each chapter all at one time.

Keep in mind these three questions as you do each study: (1) What does it *say?* (2) What does it *mean?* (3) What am I to *do* about it?

Unless you *apply* the Scriptures to your life, there is little value to be gained from knowing what it says—but when you obey God's Word, you will see growth in your life. Questions have been placed in each chapter to help you make an application of that study to your life. It is important to answer these and occasionally check previous applications to see how you are progressing in making needed changes.

A Word to Leaders

Each chapter is carefully prepared so that a leader can easily guide a group discussion. The leader should have those in his group discuss the facts learned in each section of the lesson, share what they understand them to mean, and relate what personal application then can be drawn.

He should encourage interaction by making sure that everyone has an opportunity to share, rather than allowing one person to monopolize the conversation. Require and expect that each person work through the material and fill in the blanks before the discussion time. Remember that the Bible is the sourcebook for this study, and, unless an opinion question is asked, the answer the Bible gives is the one expected. A recommended book for additional study is given at the close of each chapter. *The Myth of the Greener Grass* by J. Allan Petersen is filled with insights on marriage and how to maintain love and fidelity.

$\mathcal{I}$ now pronounce you husband and wife. . . . "

This announcement marks the end of the marriage ceremony and the beginning of married life.

Unfortunately, marriage is often entered into without serious thought and commitment, and the results can be disastrous to both persons. A decision of such far-reaching importance should be made deliberately, positively, and with the support and counsel of others—not as a reaction to a crisis, a problem, or a pressing personal need.

I know Jim and Judy well—a sharp-looking teenage couple but struggling with several difficulties. Both came from divorced families. Judy felt very alone and insecure, and loved the attention dating Jim was providing. Her deepest desire was to someday marry and have children. Jim was somewhat rebellious, felt betrayed by his parents, and was out to prove he was his own man. When Judy became pregnant, everything broke loose. The embarrassed parents insisted they hurry into marriage.

Analyze this brief history of Jim and Judy and see if you can identify ten mistakes in their marred beginning.

_____

_____

_____

_____

_____

_____

_____

_____

_____

We want to explore various important aspects of marriage, especially from a biblical point of view. Whether or not you decide to marry, you will know what God, its Designer, has to say about it.

Motivation

1. People have a variety of reasons for wanting to get married. Some reasons may be more important to one sex than to the other.

a. List below what you think some of these are.
b. Then note whether you feel each one you listed
   is of greater importance to one sex or is of the
   same priority to both males and females.
c. Rate these reasons as either "good" or "poor"
   ones for desiring to get married.

Reason	Male	Female	Both	Good	Poor
_____	☐	☐	☐	☐	☐
_____	☐	☐	☐	☐	☐
_____	☐	☐	☐	☐	☐
_____	☐	☐	☐	☐	☐
_____	☐	☐	☐	☐	☐
_____	☐	☐	☐	☐	☐
_____	☐	☐	☐	☐	☐
_____	☐	☐	☐	☐	☐

2. If you contemplate marriage in the future, which of
   the above reasons are especially important to you?

   _____

   _____

   _____

Most young men and women will someday get married. The Scriptures indicate that marriage is generally God's plan for his people. However, it is also apparent that marriage is not God's plan for everyone.

3. First Corinthians 7 deals realistically with some of the advantages and disadvantages of married life. It is intended to help answer the question of whether a Christian should marry or remain single.

   What conclusions do you draw from the following verses?

> I wish that all men were as I am. But each man has his own gift from God; one has this gift, another has that. (I Corinthians 7:7)

_____

_____

_____

> Now to the unmarried and the widows I say: It is good for them to stay unmarried, as I am. But if they cannot control themselves, they should marry, for it is better to marry than to burn with passion. (I Corinthians 7:8-9)

_____

_____

_____

> But if you do marry, you have not sinned; and if a virgin marries, she has not sinned. But those who marry will face many troubles in this life, and I want to spare you this. (I Corinthians 7:28)

_____

_____

_____

I would like you to be free from concern. An unmarried man is concerned about the Lord's affairs—how he can please the Lord. But a married man is concerned about the affairs of this world—how he can please his wife—and his interests are divided. An unmarried woman or virgin is concerned about the Lord's affairs: Her aim is to be devoted to the Lord in both body and spirit. But a married woman is concerned about the affairs of this world—how she can please her husband. I am saying this for your own good, not to restrict you, but that you may live in a right way in undivided devotion to the Lord. (1 Corinthians 7:32-35)

_____

_____

_____

_____

4. **What does the following verse indicate regarding the marital status of some of the New Testament leaders?**

Don't we have the right to take a believing wife along with us, as do the other apostles and the Lord's brothers and Cephas? (1 Corinthians 9:5)

a. Apostles

b. The Lord's brothers

c. Peter (Cephas)

5. What is the attitude toward marriage expressed in the following verse?

> Marriage should be honored by all, and the marriage bed kept pure, for God will judge the adulterer and all the sexually immoral. (Hebrews 13:4)

_____

_____

The Scriptures

The Scriptures contain clear teaching about marriage and family life. There are no pat answers, no simple formulas; but when one follows the instructions and principles given by God (who ordained marriage in the first place), then it is possible to prepare for the kind of relationships that give personal fulfillment and provide a solid, happy, and well-functioning family unit.

See what insights you can gain from the following passages concerning the beginning of marriage.

1. Read the following verses from Genesis 2:18-25:

> [18]The Lord God said, "It is not good for the man to be alone. I will make a helper suitable for him."
>
> [19]Now the Lord God had formed out of the ground all the beasts of the field and all the birds of the air. He brought them to the man to see what he would name them; and whatever the man called each living creature, that was its name. [20]So the man gave names to all the

livestock, the birds of the air and all the beasts of the field.

But for Adam no suitable helper was found. [21]So the Lord God caused the man to fall into a deep sleep; and while he was sleeping, he took one of the man's ribs and closed up the place with flesh. [22]Then the Lord God made a woman from the rib he had taken out of the man, and he brought her to the man.

[23]The man said, "This is now bone of my bones and flesh of my flesh; she shall be called 'woman,' for she was taken out of man." [24]For this reason a man will leave his father and mother and be united to his wife, and they will become one flesh.

[25]The man and his wife were both naked, and they felt no shame.

2. Give particular thought to verses 18, 23, and 24, and then answer the following:

a. Who said it was not good that man should be alone?

_____

b. Loneliness is the first thing that God named "not good." What did he do about it?

_____

_____

c. Genesis 2:18 in the King James Version translates "a helper suitable for him" as "a help meet," meaning basically "helper." What do you understand that expression to mean?

_____

_____

d. The Revised Standard Version of the Bible translates verse 23 this way: "This at last is bone of my bones and flesh of my flesh; she shall be called Woman, because she was taken out of Man."

How would you describe Adam's response to the Lord God bringing Eve to him? Check the words you think are most correct—add a couple of your own.

____ Nonchalant

____ Wow!

____ Grateful

____ Disappointed

____ Mine

____ Yawn!

____ _____

e. The following statements relate to verse 24. Mark these T for true or F for false.

T F Under God, a man is to assume independent responsibility for his wife.

T F God designed marriage to be a permanent union.

   T F Each partner in the marriage is complete in herself/himself.

3. The book of Proverbs contains a collection of wise sayings about the whole of life. In Proverbs 18:22 we read:

> He who finds a wife finds what is good and receives favor from the Lord.

a. What does this verse say about the choice of a wife?

_____

b. What further insight can be gained from the following verse, found in Proverbs 19:14?

> Houses and wealth are inherited from parents, but a prudent wife is from the Lord.

_____

_____

Evaluation

On a scale of 1 for good, 2 for fair, and 3 for poor, evaluate the following to use in considering marriage.

1. _____ Counsel of those who know you, particularly your parents.

2. ____ Prayer

3. ____ My life purpose

4. ____ Family pressure or desires

5. Timing, and as it relates to the following:

    a. ____ Age

    b. ____ Schooling

    c. ____ Finances

    d. ____ My maturity

    e. ____ Maturity of potential mate

    f. ____ Christian training

    g. ____ Home situation and responsibilities

6. ____ Honest recognition of my desires

I was so encouraged after visiting with Fred and Diane! Together with Fred's parents, they spent an evening at our home. They met in a Bible study at the university and were now engaged. Each of them talked of his and her relationship with God before they met and how God had gifted them and shown them individually his plan for them. They mentioned how they both were committed to helping each other use their strengths to the best of their ability in serving God together.

To better understand each other and potential areas of difference, they were going to take two personality and temperament analysis tests and were eager to discover the results. With unusual candor they told how they were being careful not to encourage sexual temptation between them. And Diane's parents were also supportive and felt it was a wise and good match.

All the elements of a great beginning!

Application

According to God, marriage is for life! That is serious business because more than just two people are involved. Your life touches many people. No wonder then that the Bible stresses the importance of making right decisions. Here are some to consider.

1. Decide to do God's will regarding marriage.

2. Decide if you should marry. More important than the right to get married is the right to follow God's will. He has your best interests in mind.

3. Decide whom you should marry—the right one in God's plan. While Adam slept in the will of God, he brought him a partner. Pray for your prospective partner now.

4. Decide when you should marry. Before you settle on a time to marry, several practical things should be considered. The more time you take to think and

work through the following matters, the easier will be your period of adjustment afterward:

a. *Career:* Are we both agreed on our career path and our goals together?
b. *Jobs:* Are we both employed at a level where we can begin marriage with no financial crises or debts?
c. *Finances:* Are we agreed on living expenses—budget, insurance, saving, giving, etc.?
d. *Physical:* Are we both in acceptable physical shape so we will not be overwhelmed immediately with medical expenses? Have all necessary tests been given?
e. *Schooling:* Are we agreed on further education plans and how we will afford them?
f. *Spiritual:* Are we in agreement regarding our spiritual goals, growth, and present ministry?
g. *Counseling:* Have we arranged for premarital counseling sessions with our pastor or counselor? Have we considered taking other temperament and communication tests that would give us a head start in marriage?

5. Decide what areas of your life you think you need to work on to be prepared for marriage.

a. How do you plan to do this?

_____

_____

_____

_____

b. Have someone help you on these areas of your
   life that need work.

c. Whom do you plan to ask to help you in this?

_____

_____

Recommended Reading

Wright, Norman. *Before You Say I Do.* Eugene, Oreg.:
Harvest House, 1978.

LOVE &

2

HOW IT WORKS

Love is probably the most familiar word in our language. Everyone uses it and applies it to various objects, relationships, and people. However, it is probably also one of the most misunderstood words in our entire vocabulary.

Stan and Marie were college friends—not dating friends, but just buddies in the same Bible study together. He was showing off his newly acquired car—a bright red sports model. Marie exclaimed, "I love it, I love it—the color, the upholstery, the style! I'd love to go for a ride."

Afterward Stan mentioned a recent letter from his mother and how she had gone out of her way to help the neighbors who were having some severe struggles in their family. "She really loves people," he commented. "She reaches out to everyone she can find."

Always candid in their conversations, Marie asked a tough question before they parted. "Stan, my girlfriend and I were discussing this last night: What's wrong with sex before marriage? What do you think of making love if you love someone?"

In your own words, explain the difference in the meaning of the various uses of the word *love* in their conversation.

_____

_____

_____

_____

Love Defined
....

Someone has said that love is not definable, just livable—but try.

1. What do you think? Write your own definition of *love*.

_____

_____

2. How does the dictionary define *love?* (If possible, get a contrast between old and new dictionaries.)

_____

_____

3. Explain your understanding of the difference between love and infatuation.

_____

_____

The English word *love* is used to convey many different ideas. We speak of "loving" ice cream, dogs, God, and people. As we hear the word in context, we ascribe proper meaning to it. The Greek language, in which the New Testament was written, with its four words for *love*, opens the possibility of a closer categorization.

These words and their definitions are listed below:

Stergo

This kind of love is inherent in one's own nature. It is an instinctive, natural affection or protectiveness, such as animal protectiveness for its offspring. There is a sense of responsibility for the welfare and well-being of another because of obligation in the natural, not moral, sense. This kind of love is the binding factor by which any natural or social unit is held together.

From the examples of *stergo* love given below, can you recall a specific instance that occurred in your family? (Perhaps you can think of one not listed.) Give a brief statement about one of them.

- Mother's care for sick family members.
- Father's providing for family.
- Children in a family defending one another to others outside family.

- Mother's reluctance to have her children become independent of her and leave home.

_____

_____

_____

Eros

This love is primarily based in the physical, triggered by emotion. It can easily be a self-centered love, love turned inward, wanting something in return for what it gives. It can be passion seeking self-gratification, with the tendency to exploit and take advantage of someone for personal ends.

This is the kind of "love" promoted by most Hollywood movies and TV programs in our sex-saturated society. Sexual passions are aroused with little unselfish regard for the welfare or benefit of the partner—the Playboy philosophy. In real love you want the other person's good. In erotic love you want the other person.

There is a physical, sexual basis to human love, which when controlled by Jesus Christ contributes a deep, rich meaning to life.

In marriage, sex can act as reinforcing steel does to concrete to help build a strong, solid marriage relationship.

Without a commitment to God, sex can be like a wedge to drive people apart and build deep-seated resentments, frustrations, and bitterness in a person's life.

1. Too often men and women do not exercise responsibility in their dating behavior and arouse sexual impulses rather than controlling them. What are some ways to prevent sexually arousing situations?

   a. Avoid wearing immodest clothing.

   b. _____

   c. _____

   d. _____

   e. _____

2. In the marriage relationship, a husband and wife can find the deep rich enjoyment of sex that God intended for life partners. Physical desire and fulfillment are an important part of this permanent relationship of oneness.

   The Scriptures make clear this physical joining is part of a *total* relationship and is to take place *after* the marriage has been entered into.

   a. What instruction is given in the following passage, 1 Corinthians 6:16-19, concerning intercourse outside of marriage?

   Do you not know that he who unites himself with a prostitute is one with her in body? For it is said, "The two will become one flesh." But he who unites himself with the Lord is one with him in spirit. Flee from sexual immorality. All other sins a man commits are outside his body, but he who sins sexually sins against his own body.

Do you not know that your body is a temple of the Holy
Spirit, who is in you, whom you have received from God?
You are not your own.

_____

_____.

b. **The following passage, Ephesians 5:31-32, refers
not only to a total union of persons but particularly to the sexual union. To what is this oneness
likened?**

"For this reason a man will leave his father and mother
and be united to his wife, and the two will become one
flesh." This is a profound mystery—but I am talking about
Christ and the church.

_____

_____

c. **How does the following passage, Proverbs 5:18-
19, portray the sexual aspect of marriage?**

May your fountain be blessed, and may you rejoice in the
wife of your youth. A loving doe, a graceful deer—may
her breasts satisfy you always, may you ever be capti-
vated by her love.

_____

_____

_____

d. What are some ways *eros* can be utilized to keep excitement in a marriage?

_____

_____

Phileo

This kind of love is the response of the human spirit to what appeals to it as enjoyable. It is based upon an inner communion and a mutual attraction between the person loving and the person loved. Both have things in common with each other—a similarity of outlook on life. The one loving finds a reflection of his own nature in the person loved. *Phileo* is a love of "liking" and "fondness"—a going out of the heart in delight to that which affords pleasure. The Greeks made much of friendship, and this word was used by them to designate mutual affection, as we feel toward a person who is "fun to be with." *Phileo* quality of love is important in marriage simply because we need to like someone and what they are and do, or living with them in an enduring relationship would be untenable.

Give a few examples of how *phileo* love fits in your home and in marriages that you have observed.

_____

_____

_____

_____

Agape

A love called out of one's heart by an awakened sense of the value of the object loved causes one to prize it. This volitional kind of love does not seek anything in return, not even acceptance of itself, but rather is first concerned for the other. It is a self-sacrificing love and in its absolute form denotes God's love—not human love. *Agape* is the rich word used predominantly in the New Testament to describe the love of God toward men (John 3:16), and the love that Christians are to have for each other, as illustrated by the love a man has for his wife (Ephesians 5:25).

> For God so loved the world that he gave his one and only Son, that whoever believes in him shall not perish but have eternal life. (John 3:16)

> Husbands, love your wives, just as Christ loved the church and gave himself up for her. (Ephesians 5:25)

In the Christian sense, it is a spontaneous, uncaused, self-giving love. The crucifixion of Christ is regarded as the supreme manifestation of God's love in that Christ died for helpless, sinful, unworthy man (Romans 5:5-8).

> And hope does not disappoint us, because God has poured out his love into our hearts by the Holy Spirit, whom he has given us. You see, at just the right time, when we were still powerless, Christ died for the ungodly. Very rarely will anyone die for a righteous man, though for a good man someone might possibly dare to

die. But God demonstrates his own love for us in this:
While we were still sinners, Christ died for us.
(Romans 5:5-8)

While *eros* love is often motivated by "What can I
get?" *agape* love is motivated by "What can I give?"
and finds that "it is more blessed to give than to
receive."

Have you seen evidences of *agape* love in any of
your relationships this past week? Explain.

_____

_____

_____

Obviously we cannot split love into four independent segments, for these are not necessarily exclu-
sive of each other, but there is an interplay of all in
most experiences of love.

Love Illustrated

Having faced the difficulties of defining what love is,
we recognize that love is more than a thing or an emotion. Love is a creative force that is revealed in action.

The following should challenge your thinking as to
how you can better express love and fulfill your responsibilities as one who loves.

Here are four important principles recommended by
Dr. Ed Wheat that will help you understand love and

how to make it work in your relationship. These will also offset common misconceptions you may have.

> *I can learn what love is from the Word of God.* It is rational, not irrational. I can understand love and grow in the understanding of it throughout my lifetime.

> *Love is not easy or simple.* It is an art that I must want to learn and pour my life into. I can learn how to love.

> *Love is an active power.* I control it by my own will. I am not the helpless slave of love. I can choose to love.

> *Love is the power that will produce love* as I learn to give it rather than strain to attract it.

Consider these principles with your partner and discuss any thoughts or questions prompted by them.

The Bible defines love by actions. "Little children, let us stop just *saying* we love people; let us *really* love them, and *show* it by our *actions* (1 John 3:18, TLB).

1. What did God's love prompt him to do as recorded in John 3:16?

> For God so loved the world that he gave his one and only Son, that whoever believes in him shall not perish but have eternal life.

_____

_____

2. How was God's love shown to us according to Romans 5:8?

> But God demonstrates his own love for us in this: While we were still sinners, Christ died for us.

_____

_____

3. Read 1 Corinthians 13, the love *(agape)* chapter of the New Testament.

> ¹If I speak in the tongues of men and of angels, but have not love, I am only a resounding gong or a clanging cymbal. ²If I have the gift of prophecy and can fathom all mysteries and all knowledge, and if I have a faith that can move mountains, but have not love, I am nothing. ³If I give all I possess to the poor and surrender my body to the flames, but have not love, I gain nothing.
>
> ⁴Love is patient, love is kind. It does not envy, it does not boast, it is not proud. ⁵It is not rude, it is not self-seeking, it is not easily angered, it keeps no record of wrongs. ⁶Love does not delight in evil but rejoices with the truth. ⁷It always protects, always trusts, always hopes, always perseveres.
>
> ⁸Love never fails. But where there are prophecies, they will cease; where there are tongues, they will be stilled; where there is knowledge, it will pass away. ⁹For we know in part and we prophesy in part, ¹⁰but when perfection comes, the imperfect disappears. ¹¹When I was a child, I talked like a child, I thought like a child, I

reasoned like a child. When I became a man, I put childish ways behind me.

[12]Now we see but a poor reflection as in a mirror; then we shall see face to face. Now I know in part; then I shall know fully, even as I am fully known.

[13]And now these three remain: faith, hope and love. But the greatest of these is love.

Verses 4-7 list nine ingredients of what someone has called the "spectrum of love." Consider each one and then give an example of personal failure or recent victory in your life.

a. Love is patient—longsuffering

_____

_____

_____

b. Is kind—kindness

_____

_____

_____

c. Does not envy—generosity

_____

_____

_____

d. Does not boast, is not proud—humility

_____

_____

_____

e. Is not rude—courtesy

_____

_____

_____

f. Is not self-seeking—unselfishness

_____

_____

_____

g. Is not easily angered—good tempered

_____

_____

_____

h. Does not delight in evil—guilelessness

_____

_____

_____

i. Rejoices in the truth—sincerity

_____

_____

_____

Application

These elements of love are practical in their application. You can see how well you measure up and how you are progressing. What you learn and put into practice now will greatly determine the quality and enjoyment of your marriage relationship. Think back through the things in the section "Love Illustrated." Which one do you need to work on most?

What is one practical day-by-day way you can do this?

_____

_____

_____

What form of checkup are you planning to ensure you do it?

_____

_____

_____

Summary

1. *Love is a basic essential to everyone.* We must be loved to feel significant, protected, and fulfilled. Love is the most desired commodity in the world. Anthropologist Ashley Montagu stated, "The most critical of all human needs and abilities is the need and ability to love. Of the thirty-one basic behavioral needs, it is the central, the cardinal of all the needs of human kind."

2. *Love is learned.* No one is born a lover. A baby must be loved in order to learn to love. We are born with a capacity to love but not the innate ability. Love is learned primarily at home in a harmonious, loving family. The home is the school, the laboratory where love is taught, demonstrated, and modeled.

   > Love is the only emotion that isn't natural, the only one that has to be learned, and the only one that matters. Anger, hate, and guilt blossom in the bassinet while love, sympathy, and tact require decades of steady tutelage.[1]

3. *Love must be expressed.* Love is not a secret, silent feeling that lives and dies inside of you. It is not a passive emotion that never finds expression. Kind words, generous deed, unhurried time, and warm touches are the expressions that make love authentic and believable. Love is an unselfish activity directed toward another person. "By this all men will know that you are my disciples, if you love one

another" (John 13:35). So, Christ said real love has an expression that can be seen and recognized by others around us.

4. *Each one has a unique love language.* There is little communication if you cannot speak or understand another's language. Each person is born with differing physical and emotional characteristics, personality type, and temperament traits. Add to this each one's unique home history of interacting with family members, and you've got two people who are fundamentally different. Neither is abnormal or right or wrong. Each responds in a different way to various expressions of love given by the other. Each has a unique love language that must be learned. The big question is not whether we love our mate, but how we learned to express that love in a way the other can understand and receive.

5. *Love is something we do*—a decision, a choice, a matter of the will. To love is commanded in the Bible; so it is something that can be done, an action we initiate. We cannot control every feeling, but we can control what we do. Love is not a victim of our emotions but a servant of our will. Therefore, we must act ourselves into a new way of feeling instead of trying to feel ourselves into a new way of acting.

Love is not static but dynamic, and, as such, it must grow and mature or it will diminish through neglect. As a person practices a musical instrument or practices a sport until it becomes a part of them, so "let us practice loving each other, for love comes from God and those who are loving and kind show that they are the children of God" (1 John 4:7, TLB).

Recommended Reading

Wheat, Ed. *Love Life*. Grand Rapids: Zondervan, 1980.

Notes

[1] June Callwood, *Love, Hate, Fear, Anger* (New York: Doubleday, 1964), 3.

PREPARING FOR MARRIAGE

3

*M*arriage is a unique relationship between a man and a woman through which both seek to give and receive satisfaction of their needs. Though marriage is the most significant human relationship of our life, often less time is given to preparing for it than we give to learning to drive, planning a vacation, or learning a language.

Marriage requires a level of maturity that includes willingness to assume responsibility for our actions and for our own welfare, plus the welfare of a mate and children. A young person contemplating marriage ought to be mature enough to determine his or her reasons for wanting to marry in order to judge correctly whether those reasons are adequate. A girl who rushes into marriage to escape an unhappy home life isn't acting responsibly. Nor is the man and woman who do not love each other, who have nothing in common, whose dispositions clash, who come from totally different backgrounds, but who marry when the woman finds out she is pregnant. This is immature reasoning and irresponsible behavior.

Friendships

As adolescents move toward adulthood, they tend to rely increasingly upon their peers, seeking to find mutual understanding and support from them. They rely less and less upon parents and family for their emotional needs and for help in their decision making. This is within God's plan for young people to move toward adult independence and responsibility, as long as they don't become unduly independent of the God-given authority of their parents during their growing years.

As people grow and interact with others, particularly with their peers, they develop social confidence and round out their personalities.

Even in marriage, spouses need friendships outside their own relationship for a healthy marriage.

As members of the body of Christ, Christians need to have a concern for one another. First Corinthians 12 and Romans 12 talk about this.

One could assume, therefore, that it is important to maintain friendships at every stage of life.

1. The following verse describes the development of Jesus:

And Jesus grew in wisdom and stature, and in favor with God and men. (Luke 2:52)

According to this passage, Jesus Christ increased in wisdom (mentally), stature (physically), and in favor with God (spiritually) and _____ (_____).

2. **The following verses tell us that Jesus had friends:**

Now a man named Lazarus was sick. He was from Bethany, the village of Mary and her sister Martha. This Mary, whose brother Lazarus now lay sick, was the same one who poured perfume on the Lord and wiped his feet with her hair. So the sisters sent word to Jesus, "Lord, the one you love is sick." When he heard this, Jesus said, "This sickness will not end in death. No, it is for God's glory so that God's Son may be glorified through it." Jesus loved Martha and her sister and Lazarus. (John 11:1-5)

Who were three of Jesus' friends in Bethany?
_____, _____, and _____

3. **What does the following passage say is the mark of a true friend?**

A friend loves at all times, and a brother is born for adversity. (Proverbs 17:17)

_____

_____

4. The richness of the friendship between David and
   Jonathan is recorded in 1 Samuel 18:1-4. What are
   the marks of this friendship?

   > After David had finished talking with Saul, Jonathan
   > became one in spirit with David, and he loved him as
   > himself. From that day Saul kept David with him and did
   > not let him return to his father's house. And Jonathan
   > made a covenant with David because he loved him as
   > himself. Jonathan took off the robe he was wearing and
   > gave it to David, along with his tunic, and even his sword,
   > his bow and his belt.

   _____

   _____

   Do you have or have you had a friend of the
   same sex that you feel was this kind of friend?

5. According to the following verses from Ecclesiastes,
   what are two benefits of having a close friend?

   > Two are better than one, because they have a good
   > return for their work: If one falls down, his friend can help
   > him up. But pity the man who falls and has no one to help
   > him up! (Ecclesiastes 4:9-10)

   a. _____

   b. _____

   The detriment to being a loner in life is . . . (Answer
   in your own words.)

_____

_____

_____

Casual friendships with the opposite sex are a natural way to further acquaintances, which could lead to dating and perhaps to one specific person. But remember, God has given you many brothers and sisters in Christ with whom you can have fellowship.

Dating

In our society, dating is generally the beginning of the process that leads to mate selection and marriage. Thus it is wise to think through motives and standards for dating and arrive at biblical principles that will guide the Christian in the process.

Why Date?

1. Read the list below and put a check before each phrase you think is a good reason for dating.

_____ Getting to know people of varied types, gifts, and backgrounds

_____ Gaining sex experience through experimentation

_____ Developing quality relationships with the opposite sex

_____ Discovering what your needs are for a mate

_____ Acquiring as many ego-building, romantic relationships as possible

_____ Influencing the other person (and vice versa)
in such a way that both of you will mature in
Christ

As a young person develops friendships with both
sexes, he will learn to better accept who he is and his
own sexuality. He will also learn to appreciate and understand the difference in masculine and feminine
points of view and become sensitive to the needs and
desires of the opposite sex—all within the framework
of God's guidelines.

2. At this point, it is well to consider the need to grow
   in understanding of the opposite sex. In personality
   characteristics, both sexes generally are alike; but
   there are some characteristics that tend to be more
   masculine or feminine. When a man and woman
   marry, they must unite two lives and utilize their differences to have a fully successful marriage with
   both mates finding fulfillment.

   In the following listing, place a check mark by
   the ones you have observed, realizing that these
   would be generalities.

The Man	*The Woman*
a. _ Thinks in objective way—sees the whole picture	a. _ Thinks in subjective way—in the immediate

b. _ Tends to be more
   conservative and
   deliberate in his
   decision making

b. _ Relies more on
   insights and emo-
   tions—tends toward
   impulsive actions

c. _ Prefers general ideas

c. _ Is interested in
   details

d. _ Tends to communi-
   cate to express facts
   and information

d. _ Tends to communi-
   cate to express
   feelings

e. _ Focuses on vocation

e. _ Focuses on relation-
   ship with husband
   and family

f. _ Thinks sexual love
   is a segment in life

f. _ Thinks sexual love
   is a part of the
   whole of life

g. _ Does not necessarily
   associate sex with
   love

g. _ Associates sex with
   love

3. Assuming the above to be true, how would each
   partner complete the other in each of the areas
   given above? State either your opinion of how you
   think this would work, or give an example from
   your observations of people.

a. _____

   _____

b. _____

   _____

c. _____

_____

d. _____

_____

e. _____

_____

f. _____

_____

g. _____

_____

Whom to Date

It has been said that a person ought not seriously date a person he or she would not marry.

1. Read the following passage, 2 Corinthians 6:14-18.

> [14]Do not be yoked together with unbelievers. For what do righteousness and wickedness have in common? Or what fellowship can light have with darkness? [15]What harmony is there between Christ and Belial? What does a believer have in common with an unbeliever? [16]What agreement is there between the temple of God and idols? For we are the temple of the living God. As God has said: "I will live with them and walk among them, and I will be their God, and they will be my people."
>
> [17]"Therefore come out from them and be separate,

says the Lord. Touch no unclean thing, and I will receive you."

¹⁸"I will be a Father to you, and you will be my sons and daughters, says the Lord Almighty."

What is the strong command given in verse 14?

_____

2. **What reason does the following passage, Deuteronomy 7:3-4, give for God strictly forbidding marriage between believers and unbelievers?**

> Do not intermarry with them. Do not give your daughters to their sons or take their daughters for your sons, for they will turn your sons away from following me to serve other gods, and the Lord's anger will burn against you and will quickly destroy you.

_____

_____

3. **When a person becomes a Christian, he receives a new life, a new nature, and wants to please God. Though he still struggles with some of the human desires and temptations of his former life, his new life can be cultivated and he can become spiritually strong:**

> Through these he has given us his very great and precious promises, so that through them you may participate in the divine nature and escape the corruption in the world caused by evil desires. (2 Peter 1:4)

We have not received the spirit of the world but the Spirit who is from God, that we may understand what God has freely given us. This is what we speak, not in words taught us by human wisdom but in words taught by the Spirit, expressing spiritual truths in spiritual words. The man without the Spirit does not accept the things that come from the Spirit of God, for they are foolishness to him, and he cannot understand them, because they are spiritually discerned. (1 Corinthians 2:12-14).

In the same way, count yourselves dead to sin but alive to God in Christ Jesus. Therefore do not let sin reign in your mortal body so that you obey its evil desires. Do not offer the parts of your body to sin, as instruments of wickedness, but rather offer yourselves to God, as those who have been brought from death to life; and offer the parts of your body to him as instruments of righteousness. For sin shall not be your master, because you are not under law, but under grace. What then? Shall we sin because we are not under law but under grace? By no means! Don't you know that when you offer yourselves to someone to obey him as slaves, you are slaves to the one whom you obey—whether you are slaves to sin, which leads to death, or to obedience, which leads to righteousness? (Romans 6:11-16.)

A non-Christian has only an unredeemed nature that cannot please God.

The marriage of a Christian to a non-Christian joins two people who cannot relate on the same spiritual level and increases the conflicts and misunderstandings. Such conflicts are seldom resolved, and the Christian often compromises his convictions for the sake of harmony.

What problems for the partners and their children can you foresee in such a marriage?

_____

_____

_____

How to Date
The best goal to have in all your actions in life is found in 1 Corinthians 10:31:

> Do all to the glory of God.

1. State briefly how this principle can affect a dating relationship.

   _____

   _____

   _____

2. What exhortation was given to Timothy for his relationship with the opposite sex?

   > Treat younger men as brothers, older women as mothers, and younger women as sisters, with absolute purity. (1 Timothy 5:1-2)

   _____

3. Read Genesis 26:6-11 and note the action that betrayed Isaac's attempt to pass Rebecca off as his sister.

> So Isaac stayed in Gerar. When the men of that place asked him about his wife, he said, "She is my sister," because he was afraid to say, "She is my wife." He thought, "The men of this place might kill me on account of Rebekah, because she is beautiful." When Isaac had been there a long time, Abimelech king of the Philistines looked down from a window and saw Isaac caressing his wife Rebekah. So Abimelech summoned Isaac and said, "She is really your wife! Why did you say, 'She is my sister'?" Isaac answered him, "Because I thought I might lose my life on account of her." Then Abimelech said, "What is this you have done to us? One of the men might well have slept with your wife, and you would have brought guilt upon us." So Abimelech gave orders to all the people: "Anyone who molests this man or his wife shall surely be put to death."

a. How did Abimelech know he had been lied to?

_____

_____

b. If someone were to observe your normal dating behavior what conclusions would they draw?

_____ That you are brother and sister

____ That you have more than a casual interest in one another

____ That you are married

____ That you belong to Christ

4. Dating as Christians involves being an example to each other in Christ-likeness.

a. What principle from the life of Jesus is given in the following passage of Scripture?

> For even the Son of Man did not come to be served, but to serve, and to give his life as a ransom for many. (Mark 10:45)

_____

b. State how you think this principle can be applied to your dating responsibilities:

_____

_____

As you find your dating is leading to more serious thoughts of possible engagement, these are some practical questions you should ask yourself regarding your potential mate:

- Do other members of your mate's sex like him or her? Members of the opposite sex?
- What does your mate talk about? Does the personal pronoun dominate the conversation?

- Is your mate poised or on the defensive?
- Is your mate interested in others?
- Is your mate scrupulously honest in the handling of money? Is your mate more interested in earning money than in having it given to him or her?
- What about your mate's sense of responsibility? Does he or she keep appointments? Does he or she respect the rights and property of others?
- Does your mate have a sense of honor? tell the truth? Can you count on him or her?
- Do you have a good time together without too much emphasis on sex? Do you have a good feeling the next morning after you have been together the night before?
- What are the things at which your mate gets angry?
- What are the things your mate thinks are funny?
- Does your mate have high ideals? Does he or she have a selfish or unselfish purpose in life?
- Can you be proud of your mate in front of your friends? your parents?
- Is your mate willing to work? Does he or she show more interest in the job than in the pay? in what is accomplished more than the credit?
- In playing games can your mate win without gloating or lose without sulking? Do you always have to do what he or she wants to do?
- Does a commitment to Christ really mean something important to your mate? Is your mate

doing things that help him or her grow spiritually?

Engagement

Often dating leads to a deepening interest, that leads to a *committal* of love—recognizing that God is leading the two of you to marriage, to share life together.

The time of waiting to be married, the time called the engagement period, should be a wonderful learning experience for the future couple. It is a time for each to learn more about himself and about his mate.

1. An invaluable aid for an engaged couple as they prepare for marriage is to study the marriages of their parents. The kind of relationship they have had as husband and wife greatly influence their children.

   Research studies have found that when both partners come from happy homes, their chances of making a good adjustment to each other are more than twice as good as those from unhappy or even average families.

Your Parents:

a. What are the personal characteristics of your mother?_____

_____

Your father? _____

_____

b. What do you see to be areas of strength in their marriage?

_____

_____

Areas of failure? _____

_____

c. Answer yes or no to the following questions:

____ Do your parents put each other first?

____ Who was the leader in the marriage?

____ Do they listen to each other?

____ Is their marriage growing?

____ Do they compliment each other and say "thank you"?

d. What negative traits have you picked up from your parents?

_____

_____

Your Prospective Partner's Parents:

a. If you are engaged, do you know the parents of your fianceé?

b. is your partner following or repudiating the family patterns?

2. Only God can meet a person's total needs . . . in marriage or out of it! This means that a couple ought to be continually growing in their relationship to Christ.

Are you maturing as a Christian in the following areas? Answer yes or no.

____ Putting priority on daily time alone with God.

____ Talking freely to others about Christ.

____ Being sensitive to the sin in your life and dealing with it.

____ Increasing in obedience to the Word of God.

3. Matthew 1:18-25 records the announcement to Joseph and Mary about the coming birth of Jesus:

> This is how the birth of Jesus Christ came about: His mother Mary was pledged to be married to Joseph, but before they came together, she was found to be with child through the Holy Spirit. Because Joseph her husband was a righteous man and did not want to expose her to public disgrace, he had in mind to divorce her quietly. But after he had considered this, an angel of the Lord appeared to him in a dream and said, "Joseph son of David, do not be afraid to take Mary home as your wife, because what is conceived in her is from the Holy Spirit. She will give birth to a son, and you are to give him the name Jesus, because he will save his people from their sins." All this took place to fulfill what the Lord had said through the prophet: "The virgin will be with child and will give birth to a son, and they will call him Immanuel" —which means, "God with us." When Joseph

woke up, he did what the angel of the Lord had commanded him and took Mary home as his wife. But he had no union with her until she gave birth to a son. And he gave him the name Jesus.

a. What was their relationship?

b. Even though they were committed to each other but were not married, how did they behave themselves sexually? _____

_____

c. Did Joseph treat her with respect ____ or disdain ____ or rejection ____ ?

d. How did Joseph indicate his desire to obey God?

_____

_____

4. Jacob and Rachel's engagement story is told in Genesis 29:18-21.

> [18]Jacob was in love with Rachel and said, "I'll work for you seven years in return for your younger daughter Rachel."
>
> [19]Laban said, "It's better that I give her to you than to some other man. Stay here with me." [20]So Jacob served seven years to get Rachel, but they seemed like only a few days to him because of his love for her.
>
> [21]Then Jacob said to Laban, "Give me my wife. My time is completed, and I want to lie with her."

a. How would you describe Jacob's love for Rachel?

_____

b. Even though it was a long engagement (to put it mildly!) what was Jacob's reaction?

_____

_____

c. What was their sexual relationship during this time? See verse 21.

_____

Application

What will God have you to do as a result of what you have learned in this lesson?

1. Write down things you feel are especially important as you look for God's leading in selecting a mate.

_____

_____

_____

2. List the things you want to establish in your relationship with the opposite sex to make sure you are pleasing God . . .

a. In friendships

_____

_____

b. In dating

_____

_____

_____

c. In engagement

_____

_____

_____

Summary

If marriage is in God's plan for a person, God can certainly lead that one to an equally dedicated person that will be suitable as a marriage partner. But that doesn't guarantee a trouble-free relationship. No one would suggest that God brought Adam and Eve together, but that didn't ensure family success.

To say, "We're made for each other" has dangerous and unrealistic overtones. It has the thought that we are completely compatible, our personalities are a perfect match, and we will not have the difficulties and adjustments other couples have. Not so—never! We may be *meant* for each other and believe our marriage was made in heaven. But all the maintenance work is done on earth.

Concluding Thoughts and Questions

Why am I marrying this person?

If this person had no sexual appeal to me, would I still feel that he or she would make a good friend whose companionship I would enjoy and whose conversations wouldn't bore me?

Will this person make a good parent for my children?

> If you are contemplating marriage because you are lonely, bored, afraid, frustrated, pregnant, or embarrassed to be the unmarried one among your friends, then it would be wise for you to give serious thought to whether you should continue the engagement. The only valid reason for anyone to get married is "because I believe God wants me to spend the rest of my life with this person whom I love and respect and these are his/her reasons also."

> This means exactly what it says—the rest of our life. Not "til misunderstandings do us part," or until he or she loses physical attractiveness, or until I find someone better, or until I'm tired of

responsibility and decide to enjoy my freedom
(Dr. Anthony Florio).

Recommended Reading

Warren, Neil Clark. *Finding the Love of Your Life*. Focus
on the Family, 1992.

ACCEPTING
4
YOURSELF & OTHERS

A pastor's wife told me the incredible story of her pathetic home history. Her parents had the strange idea that children come equipped with wisdom, motivation, and good judgment. When as a small girl she would ask for some help with a school assignment, her mother would respond, "If you're too dumb to figure it out yourself, you don't need to understand it. You're stupid!" During the girl's high school years the mother repeatedly reminded her, "You'll never have a boyfriend—no one would want to date you—no man will ever marry you." Since the daughter married, the angry mother has refused to let her return home for a visit but welcomes her husband, the son-in-law.

Questions: How can this woman who has been taught that she is unloved, worthless, and incapable have an unselfish, outgoing love for others? If she does not believe that she is an important person, made in the image of God, how can she believe that about her husband and treat him as such? How can she give what she doesn't have? How could she want to give love to a marriage partner if she didn't feel she had something to give—or that anyone would want her love?

If you don't have a healthy self-acceptance, how can you expect your mate to accept you for who you are? You'll continually try to prove yourself to him or her and be less likely to achieve a meaningful relationship. Either you will be apprehensive about encountering others for fear of rejection or you will attack others as a way to cover your own sense of inferiority.

Self-Acceptance

A person with any degree of honesty knows he has done wrong things, needs forgiveness, and has much room for improvement in his life. However, it is also true that unless you have a healthy *self-love* you cannot adequately love others.

1. The Bible clearly states that a man has a relationship to himself as well as to God and others. Read how Jesus expressed this in the following passage, Mark 12:28-34:

   > [28]One of the teachers of the law came and heard them debating. Noticing that Jesus had given them a good answer, he asked him, "Of all the commandments, which is the most important?"
   >
   > [29]"The most important one," answered Jesus, "is this:

'Hear, O Israel, the Lord our God, the Lord is one. [30]Love the Lord your God with all your heart and with all your soul and with all your mind and with all your strength.' [31]The second is this: 'Love your neighbor as yourself.' There is no commandment greater than these."

[32]"Well said, teacher," the man replied. "You are right in saying that God is one and there is no other but him. [33]To love him with all your heart, with all your understanding and with all your strength, and to love your neighbor as yourself is more important than all burnt offerings and sacrifices."

[34]When Jesus saw that he had answered wisely, he said to him, "You are not far from the kingdom of God." And from then on no one dared ask him any more questions.

Now answer the following:

a. According to verse 31, what should one's attitude be toward himself?

_____

b. The normal human tendency seems to be to put self first and let God and others fit into life as is convenient. Another popular view is that one should love God first, others next, and self last. But Jesus gives the proper sequence in verses 30-31. What is it?

First _____

Second _____

Third _____

c. Why do you think this is a necessary order?

_____

_____

Jesus' words, "Love your neighbor as yourself" is a positive command. He was assuming man's love for himself, that God-given sense of worth and value. Created into each person is that natural appreciation, care, and protection for himself. Without this, life itself would not be desirable.

The mental picture we carry of ourself greatly affects our attitudes, emotions, and responses toward God, family, friends, job, and many other significant areas of our life.

We act like the person we conceive ourself to be. And this self-image sets the boundaries of our emotional maturity, personal achievement, and spiritual growth.

2. Read the following Scripture passage, 2 Corinthians 10:12, which speaks about self-worth:

> We do not dare to classify or compare ourselves with some who commend themselves. When they measure themselves by themselves and compare themselves with themselves, they are not wise.

What does it indicate as an unwise standard for measuring your self-worth?

_____

3. Read 1 Samuel 16:7 and see why the knowledge other people have of you is often based on incomplete information.

> But the Lord said to Samuel, "Do not consider his appearance or his height, for I have rejected him. The Lord does not look at the things man looks at. Man looks at the outward appearance, but the Lord looks at the heart."

a. What is the reason given?

_____

_____

b. In contrast, what further insight does God have about you?

_____

_____

4. There are other factors besides one's appearance that might be used to incorrectly place value upon someone's worth. Identify them as you read these Scriptures:

> When Jesus had finished these parables, he moved on from there. Coming to his hometown, he began teaching the people in their synagogue, and they were amazed. "Where did this man get this wisdom and these miraculous powers?" they asked. "Isn't this the carpenter's son? Isn't his mother's name Mary, and aren't his brothers James, Joseph, Simon and Judas? Aren't all his sisters with

us? Where then did this man get all these things?" (Matthew 13:53-56)

Philip found Nathanael and told him, "We have found the one Moses wrote about in the Law, and about whom the prophets also wrote—Jesus of Nazareth, the son of Joseph." "Nazareth! Can anything good come from there?" Nathanael asked. "Come and see," said Philip. (John 1:45-46)

This is what the Lord says: "Let not the wise man boast of his wisdom or the strong man boast of his strength or the rich man boast of his riches, but let him who boasts boast about this: that he understands and knows me, that I am the Lord, who exercises kindness, justice and righteousness on earth, for in these I delight," declares the Lord. (Jeremiah 9:23-24)

---

5. A reason for a feeling of unworthiness can be found in Luke 15:21.

The son said to him, "Father, I have sinned against heaven and against you. I am no longer worthy to be called your son."

What attitude is expressed in this verse and why?

_____

_____

_____

6. What kind of self-image did you have in your early
   teens? Using the scale of 1 as good, 2 as fair, and 3
   as poor, how would you have rated yourself in each
   area?

       I felt _____ about my parentage.

       I felt _____ about my appearance.

       I felt _____ about my abilities.

       I felt _____ about my environment.

       I felt _____ about my relationship to God.

Self-esteem is not based on the great things you've
accomplished, the mark you have made, the things
you own, nor is it canceled by your faults, failures, and
sins. These acts reveal *what* you are but do not indicate
who you are and your divine origin. Self-love and self-
approval are not the same. The true basis for a healthy
self-love is to understand and accept the value God
places on you!

7. What do the Scriptures say about your worth before
   God? Enter your response on the line following
   each Scripture.

For God so loved the world that he gave his one and only Son, that whoever believes in him shall not perish but have eternal life. (John 3:16)

_____

Cast all your anxiety on him because he cares for you. (1 Peter 5:7)

_____

The Lord appeared to us in the past, saying: "I have loved you with an everlasting love; I have drawn you with loving-kindness. (Jeremiah 31:3)

_____

As the Father has loved me, so have I loved you. Now remain in my love. (John 15:9)

_____

Man is unique! God simply spoke, and the whole universe came into being through his creative word. He did not speak man into existence, but with special care he personally formed him and endowed him with many of his own divine characteristics.

God did not create any superior or inferior people. There are only different people. Abilities and capacities differ; each person has unique strengths that enable him to make his special contribution to God's plan.

To refuse to accept yourself as God made you is actually rebellion, for unconsciously you are accusing him of making a mistake. Any kind of rebellion must be honestly faced and confessed.

8. **Genesis 1:27 states:**

> So God created man in his own image, in the image of
> God he created him; male and female he created them.

9. **Romans 5:12 explains what marred that image:**

> Sin entered the world through one man, and death
> through sin, and in this way death came to all men,
> because all sinned.

**State in your own words what it was that marred
God's image in us:**

_____

10. **Colossians 1:15-22, stated below, explains how God
restored fellowship with man:**

> [15]He is the image of the invisible God, the firstborn over
> all creation. [16]For by him all things were created: things in
> heaven and on earth, visible and invisible, whether
> thrones or powers or rulers or authorities; all things
> were created by him and for him. [17]He is before all things,
> and in him all things hold together. [18]And he is the head
> of the body, the church; he is the beginning and the
> firstborn from among the dead, so that in everything he
> might have the supremacy. [19]For God was pleased to
> have all his fullness dwell in him, [20]and through him to
> reconcile to himself all things, whether things on earth or
> things in heaven, by making peace through his blood, shed
> on the cross.
>
> [21]Once you were alienated from God and were

enemies in your minds because of your evil behavior.
²²But now he has reconciled you by Christ's physical
body through death to present you holy in his sight,
without blemish and free from accusation.

**Tell in a few words how God restored man to fel-
lowship with himself.**

_____

_____

11. Even the most gross acts of sin can be cleansed and
forgiven by Jesus Christ. Read 1 Corinthians 6:9-11,
cited below, which records some specific sins that
had been a part of the Corinthian believers' background before they became Christians:

Do you not know that the wicked will not inherit the
kingdom of God? Do not be deceived: Neither the
sexually immoral nor idolaters nor adulterers nor male
prostitutes nor homosexual offenders nor thieves nor
the greedy nor drunkards nor slanderers nor swindlers
will inherit the kingdom of God. And that is what some
of you were. But you were washed, you were sanctified,
you were justified in the name of the Lord Jesus Christ
and by the Spirit of our God.

What were some of these sins?

_____

_____

12. God desires that those who come to him should be conformed to the image of (be like) his Son. You can accept a self that is in the process of being made like Jesus! What do the Scriptures below say about this?

And we, who with unveiled faces all reflect the Lord's glory, are being transformed into his likeness with ever-increasing glory, which comes from the Lord, who is the Spirit. (2 Corinthians 3:18)

_____

_____

Do not lie to each other, since you have taken off your old self with its practices and have put on the new self, which is being renewed in knowledge in the image of its Creator. (Colossians 3:9-10)

_____

_____

Through these he has given us his very great and precious promises, so that through them you may participate in the divine nature and escape the corruption in the world caused by evil desires. (2 Peter 1:4)

_____

_____

Dear friends, now we are children of God, and what we will be has not yet been made known. But we know that when he appears, we shall be like him, for we shall see him as he is. Everyone who has this hope in him purifies himself, just as he is pure. (1 John 3:2-3)

_____

_____

The very fact that God, knowing *what* you are, provided Christ for your forgiveness proves that you are not worthless! Unworthy, yes—but never worthless. His love indicates *who* you are—one of God's important creatures in whom he has a great investment. If God so loved you, you must be a very important person!

13. Being created in God's image, you have intellect, emotion, and a will, which God housed in a body that would best achieve the purpose he has for you.

   The psalmist recognized that every man is a unique creation of God. Using Psalm 139:13-16, cited below, list how God specifically designed you.

> For you created my inmost being; you knit me together in my mother's womb. I praise you because I am fearfully and wonderfully made; your works are wonderful, I know that full well. My frame was not hidden from you when I was made in the secret place. When I was woven together in the depths of the earth, your eyes saw my unformed body. All the days ordained for me were written in your book before one of them came to be.

_____

_____

Thank God you are you!

Commit yourself to God. When you voluntarily give yourself to God for his control and use, you are recognizing your tremendous worth. You are loving yourself in the highest sense of the word.

It is not only safe, but necessary, to love whom God loves—yourself!!

Understanding Others

When you are able to accept yourself you will find you are better able to understand and be sensitive to the needs of other people.

1. What commandment did Jesus give about loving others in the following passage?

   A new command I give you: Love one another. As I have loved you, so you must love one another. By this all men will know that you are my disciples, if you love one another. (John 13:34-35)

   _____

2. If you focus on the negatives in another person's life, your love for him will be weakened. It is God's will that people love one another. The remedy to overcome lack of love is given in the following verse:

   Finally, brothers, whatever is true, whatever is noble, whatever is right, whatever is pure, whatever is lovely, whatever is admirable—if anything is excellent or praise-worthy—think about such things. (Philippians 4:8)

What does this verse say your thoughts should dwell on?

_____

_____

_____

3. According to the following passage from Romans, when someone becomes a Christian, he is responsible to God. What do these verses caution us against doing to another Christian?

You, then, why do you judge your brother? Or why do you look down on your brother? For we will all stand before God's judgment seat. It is written: "As surely as I live," says the Lord, "every knee will bow before me; every tongue will confess to God." So then, each of us will give an account of himself to God. Therefore let us stop passing judgment on one another. Instead, make up your mind not to put any stumbling block or obstacle in your brother's way. (Romans 14:10-13)

_____

_____

4. According to the following verses, how can you best be of help to other Christians?

Above all, love each other deeply, because love covers over a multitude of sins. (1 Peter 4:8)

_____

_____

Therefore confess your sins to each other and pray for each other so that you may be healed. The prayer of a righteous man is powerful and effective. (James 5:16)

_____

_____

Let us return to where we started in this chapter: "Love your neighbor as yourself." We would do well to ask what our needs are and how we would like them met.

We need to do what is right. Righteousness yields a clear conscience and liberates us from the bondage of guilt and worry and fear. We need to be forgiven. We need to be tolerated, to receive "space" for our weaknesses and frailties, without rejection or disdain. We need to be encouraged. We need to be affirmed. We need to know that we have worth and value for what God has made us by his grace. We need others to tell us the truth. Only then can we accurately understand the issues we face and make good decisions. These few words give us a significant work-sheet for loving others (Dr. Joseph Stowell).

Application

As you consider your attitude toward yourself, do you feel you have a healthy view of who you are? What will you be able to offer in marriage—maturity? responsibleness?

You have been thinking through much Scripture in this lesson. All these verses are important and can make a significant difference in your life now and help you to accept your partner when you marry.

Which ones impressed you most?

_____

_____

_____

How can you begin to apply this Scripture to your life?

_____

_____

_____

The Christian concept of marriage is based on the prerequisite that both partners in the marriage are Christians. Only the presence of Jesus Christ in a life can make carrying out his teachings possible.

At this stage in the study, you may be asking, "How does one become a Christian?" or "How can I know for sure that I am a Christian?" Good questions!

Here is a brief explanation and illustration to help answer these questions for you.

God made us with both a God-consciousness and the capability to live in a right relationship with God. Although there are a lot of good people, no one is perfect. The Bible describes this simply in Romans 3:23:

> All have sinned and come short of the glory of God.

Since sin separates (whether it be in relationship to God or to people), we live in a state of spiritual death. Romans 6:23 says:

> For the wages of sin is death.

Because God loves us and desires us to live in right relationship and fellowship with himself, he made provision for our sin.

> Christ died for sins once for all, the righteous for the unrighteous, to bring you to God. (1 Peter 3:18)

Romans 5:8 puts it this way:

> God demonstrates his own love for us in this: While we were still sinners, Christ died for us.

The following illustration shows this clearly and depicts 1 Timothy 2:5 as stated in *The Living Bible:*

> God is on one side and all the people on the other side; and Christ Jesus . . . is between them to bring them together.

MAN—imperfect, sinful, destined for spiritual death (eternal separation from God)	JESUS—the way across	GOD—holy, pure, perfect, with a perfect place prepared for us—along with an abundant life while we are here on earth.

MAN—imperfect, sinful, destined for spiritual death (eternal separation from God)

Man's efforts fall short

Ephesians 2:8-9—"For it is by grace you have been saved, through faith—and this not from yourselves, it is the gift of God—not by works, so that no one can boast."

JESUS—the way across

John 3:16—"For God so loved the world that he gave his one and only Son, that whoever believes in him shall not perish but have eternal life."

GOD—holy, pure, perfect, with a perfect place prepared for us—along with an abundant life while we are here on earth.

John 10:10—"I have come that they may have life, and have it to the full."

1 ——————➤ 2 ——————➤ 3 ——————➤ 4

The numbers above depict groups of people.

Group one includes everyone—"*All* have sinned."

Group two indicates a progression—the people in this group recognize that there probably is a God but do not do anything about it.

Group three and *four* are described by one verse, John 1:12:

> Yet to all who received him, to those who believed in his name, he gave the right to become children of God.

Group three comprises those who *believe.* That is, they acknowledge their sin, their need of a Savior, and the fact that Jesus is God in the flesh who died for them. Many people are in this group, but they have never taken the step into *group four*—those who *believe* and *receive* Christ as Savior. *Receiving* is an act of the will whereby one invites Jesus Christ into his life as Savior and Lord. How is this done? Revelation 3:20 states:

> Here I am! I stand at the door and knock. If anyone hears
> my voice and opens the door, I will come in and eat with
> him, and he with me.

It is by personal choice and invitation.

Where do you place yourself in the illustration?

If you've never invited Christ into your life or are not sure that you are a Christian, just pray this prayer:

"Lord Jesus, I'm a sinner. I know you died for my sins, and I now ask that you come into my life as my Savior and Lord. I know that when you do this, you give me your life. Thank you."

If you did this, sign your name and date it so you can look back on the exact time you became a Christian. Isn't that great! Now, on the basis of God's Word you can *know* that you have eternal life!

> And this is the testimony: God has given us eternal life,
> and this life is in his Son. He who has the Son has life; he
> who does not have the Son of God does not have life. I
> write these things to you who believe in the name of the

Son of God so that you may know that you have eternal life." (1 John 5:11-13)

Your Name _____ Date _____

Recommended Reading

McDowell, Josh. *His Image . . . My Image.* San Bernardino, Calif.: Here's Life Publishers, 1985.

COMMUNICATION

5

$\mathcal{T}$he director of a marriage counseling service said, "All across this country are husbands and wives who cannot talk to each other. This, I am convinced, is our number one marriage problem. Couples don't need a psychiatrist or a marriage counselor—they could solve their own problems if they learned to communicate."

Next to spiritual commitment and physical survival, the greatest need of a human being is to be understood, affirmed, and appreciated. Feelings grow best out of conversation. Couples must devote themselves to talking—about anything and everything—important things, mundane things, pleasant things, disturbing things. Romance begins with knowledge of one another, and the key to knowledge is open, honest, consistent communication. Therefore, learning to communicate is the most important skill in life and is necessary to succeed in any relationship. Communication is shared meaning—shared understanding.

The heart of marital oneness is the communication system. Thus, the ability to communicate well is a fundamental skill essential to the growth of the marriage relationship.

Although strong marriages tend to have the same problem areas as weak ones, those marriages that succeed apparently do so because the mates are communicating clearly.

One major study discovered that in verbal communication only 7 percent of the message is conveyed by the words themselves, 38 percent by the tone of voice, and 55 percent by facial expressions and gestures.

Ways to Communicate

People communicate in a variety of ways. Words are one means by which a person can express himself. *Action* language is another. *Silence* can convey a wealth of information! *Listening* is an indispensable condition for meaningful communication.

1. Following the examples given, list other ways you communicate verbally and nonverbally with others.

Verbally	Non-Verbally
a. *Soft Voice*	a. *With Eyes*
b. _____	b. _____
c. _____	c. _____

d. _____   d. _____

e. _____   e. _____

2. How do you think the five senses are involved in
   what is communicated between marriage partners?

   a. Sight

   _____

   _____

   b. Hearing

   _____

   _____

   c. Touch

   _____

   _____

   d. Smell

   _____

   _____

   e. Taste

   _____

   _____

Why Communicate?

Communicate: "To give or interchange thoughts, feelings, information, or the like, by writing, speaking, etc." *(Random House Dictionary of the English Language)*.

You cannot *not* communicate! Relating to others takes place by communication.

1. There are a number of levels of communication. Some of these are listed below. After each one, describe a specific instance that occurred with your family or friends last week.

   a. Casual conversation with friends

   _____

   _____

   _____

   b. Sharing of information

   _____

   _____

   _____

   c. Self-disclosure—sharing of feelings, attitudes, emotions with another person

   _____

   _____

d. Goal planning (short- or long-term)

_____

_____

_____

e. Expressions of disagreement, argument

_____

_____

_____

f. Giving support and encouragement to someone

_____

_____

_____

g. Listening to another person

_____

_____

_____

2. The importance of a married couple keeping the lines of communication open seems obvious.

Conversation meets varied needs of marriage partners. Briefly comment on the statements given below.

a. Talk establishes communication between marriage partners.

_____

_____

b. A woman generally has a greater need for communication than her husband. (It's a wise man who understands and fulfills this need!)

_____

_____

c. Usually the more time a husband and wife spend talking together, the more satisfying their marital relationship will be.

_____

_____

Marriage is intended to be an intimate relationship built upon mutual understanding between a husband and wife. For this communion of hearts to occur, conversation must go beyond the level of home and children to include a sharing of thoughts and feelings in the experiences of daily living. Do you know many marriage partners who you believe probably communicate on all of the above levels in question 1?

_____ Yes _____ No

How do you think you would do?

_____ Good _____ Fair _____ Poor

The Art of Verbal Communication

Consider the immense power of the spoken word for good or bad! It is easy to see why the Bible speaks so often concerning the importance of proper use of the tongue.

Understanding and applying these passages can improve your ability to verbally communicate with others.

1. Examine Ephesians 4:15, cited below:

> Instead, speaking the truth in love, we will in all things grow up into him who is the Head, that is, Christ.

From the listing below check the answers you feel are correct.

_____ It doesn't make much difference what you say as long as it is said lovingly.

_____ *How* you say something is important.

_____ "White lies" have a place in communication in interpersonal relationships.

_____ What and how you speak has a direct effect on maturing in Christ.

2. Ephesians 4:29, cited below, gives four principles concerning communication.

> Do not let any unwholesome talk come out of your mouths, but only what is helpful for building others up

according to their needs, that it may benefit those who listen.

Check whether you agree with the two principles given below, and list the other two?

a. Don't speak wrongly to or of another person.

____ Yes ____ No

b. What you say should help, not hinder, others.

____ Yes ____ No

c. _____

d. _____

3. What do the following passages say about *constructive* communication? Write your response on the line following each Scripture.

The Sovereign Lord has given me an instructed tongue, to know the word that sustains the weary. He wakens me morning by morning, wakens my ear to listen like one being taught. (Isaiah 50:4)

Be an encourager

"In your anger do not sin": Do not let the sun go down while you are still angry, and do not give the devil a foothold. (Ephesians 4:26-27)

_____

_____

Be kind and compassionate to one another, forgiving each other, just as in Christ God forgave you. (Ephesians 4:32)

_____

_____

Set a guard over my mouth, O Lord; keep watch over the door of my lips. (Psalm 141:3)

_____

_____

An anxious heart weighs a man down, but a kind word cheers him up. (Proverbs 12:25)

_____

_____

A gentle answer turns away wrath, but a harsh word stirs up anger. The tongue of the wise commends knowledge, but the mouth of the fool gushes folly. The eyes of the Lord are everywhere, keeping watch on the wicked and the good. The tongue that brings healing is a tree of life, but a deceitful tongue crushes the spirit. (Proverbs 15:1-4)

_____

_____

The heart of the righteous weighs its answers, but the mouth of the wicked gushes evil. (Proverbs 15:28)

_____

_____

He who guards his mouth and his tongue keeps himself from calamity. (Proverbs 21:23)

_____

_____

Barriers to Communication

1. To develop better dialogue with others, learn what interrupts effective communication.

   Read the following Scripture verses, then on the lines following each verse comment briefly on what to avoid in communication.

   A man who lacks judgment derides his neighbor, but a man of understanding holds his tongue. (Proverbs 11:12)

   _____

   _____

   A gossip betrays a confidence, but a trustworthy man keeps a secret. (Proverbs 11:13)

   _____

   _____

   A fool shows his annoyance at once, but a prudent man overlooks an insult. (Proverbs 12:16)

   _____

   _____

Reckless words pierce like a sword, but the tongue of the wise brings healing. (Proverbs 12:18)

_____

_____

The Lord detests lying lips, but he delights in men who are truthful. (Proverbs 12:22)

_____

_____

A fool finds no pleasure in understanding but delights in airing his own opinions. (Proverbs 18:2)

_____

_____

He who answers before listening—that is his folly and his shame. (Proverbs 18:13)

_____

_____

Better to live in a desert than with a quarrelsome and ill-tempered wife. (Proverbs 21:19)

_____

_____

Do you see a man who speaks in haste? There is more hope for a fool than for him. (Proverbs 29:20)

_____

_____

Take a big step in improving your communication by vowing never to make anyone the object of remarks that cut, belittle, or ridicule!

This resolve should continue when you marry, to spare your partner the devastating effects such remarks produce.

2. Anger is real!

a. Mark the following statements about anger by circling either *T* for True or *F* for False.

T F All human beings have the emotion of anger.

T F Christians are never supposed to get angry.

T F Silence can be an escape from settling angry feelings.

T F Aggressive feelings should be recognized and resolved.

b. What does James 1:19-20, cited below, say about anger?

My dear brothers, take note of this: Everyone should be quick to listen, slow to speak and slow to become angry, for man's anger does not bring about the righteous life that God desires.

_____

_____

You may disagree with others, but agree to disagree agreeably!

The Tongue

James 3:1-12 talks about the control of the tongue. Look at this passage and then answer the questions.

> [1]Not many of you should presume to be teachers, my brothers, because you know that we who teach will be judged more strictly. [2]We all stumble in many ways. If anyone is never at fault in what he says, he is a perfect man, able to keep his whole body in check.
>
> [3]When we put bits into the mouths of horses to make them obey us, we can turn the whole animal. [4]Or take ships as an example. Although they are so large and are driven by strong winds, they are steered by a very small rudder wherever the pilot wants to go. [5]Likewise the tongue is a small part of the body, but it makes great boasts. Consider what a great forest is set on fire by a small spark. [6]The tongue also is a fire, a world of evil among the parts of the body. It corrupts the whole person, sets the whole course of his life on fire, and is itself set on fire by hell.
>
> [7]All kinds of animals, birds, reptiles and creatures of the sea are being tamed and have been tamed by man, [8]but no man can tame the tongue. It is a restless evil, full of deadly poison.
>
> [9]With the tongue we praise our Lord and Father, and with it we curse men, who have been made in God's

likeness. ¹⁰Out of the same mouth come praise and cursing. My brothers, this should not be. ¹¹Can both fresh water and salt water flow from the same spring? ¹²My brothers, can a fig tree bear olives, or a grapevine bear figs? Neither can a salt spring produce fresh water.

1. To what does God compare the tongue in verses 3-6?

_____

_____

2. How is the tongue described in verses 7-8?

_____

_____

3. What is the implication in verses 9-12? Check appropriate answers.

____ To praise God and condemn man reveals inconsistency.

____ Nature exhibits many contradictions.

____ God's help is needed to control the tongue.

Application

1. In order to strengthen your communication ability, try this experiment: Mentally switch roles with a family member or close friend, and try to express that person's feelings on the basis of your present

communication relationship. Now go to that person
and let them tell you their own ideas for improving
communication.

2. Review this lesson and determine to improve one
   area of communication immediately. What is it?

   _____

   How do you propose to improve this area?

   _____

   _____

   _____

3. Positive or negative. The American Institute of Family Relations reported a survey in which parents
   were asked to record how many negative—as
   opposed to positive—comments they made to their
   children. The results? It was discovered that parents
   criticized their children ten times for every favorable
   comment. In another survey teachers were found to
   be 75 percent negative. And it was learned that it
   takes four positive statements from a teacher to offset the effects of one negative statement to a child.

   When you mine for gold, you must move tons of
   dirt to find a single ounce of gold. You do not look
   for the dirt; you look for the gold. Similarly, in
   human relations, you should become a "gold-
   finder."

Recommended Reading

Hybels, Bill and Lynne, *Fit to Be Tied*. Grand Rapids: Zondervan, 1993.

*N*o matter how many other fine traits there are in a marriage partner, a lack of thoughtful and sympathetic consideration will overshadow and sour them all. And most of what we get in marriage is self-induced. It is the immutable law of the echo. We get in return exactly what we give. What we send out comes back to us—increased.

A teacher asked her students to jot down the names of people they really disliked. Some students could think of one. Others listed as many as fourteen. The interesting fact that emerged was *those students who disliked the most people were themselves the most widely disliked.*

Jesus said it clearly: "Treat men exactly as you would like them to treat you. . . . Don't judge other people and you will not be judged yourselves. Don't condemn and you will not be condemned. Forgive others and people will forgive you. Give and men will give to you. . . . For whatever measure you use with other people, they will use in their dealings with you" (Luke 6:31, 37-38, Phillips).

So, a basic law of relationships is that you give what you need. Decide what you want from other people—understanding, gentleness, careful thought, and attention, etc.—and give these first yourself.

Consideration—What Is It?

1. What is your definition of *consideration?*

_____

_____

_____

2. How do others define it? Get an opinion from someone else. (Also, write down what others share during the study discussion time.)

_____

_____

_____

3. Name some of the ways you feel that maturity and consideration in marriage go together.

_____

_____

_____

4. List some of the evidences of consideration that you feel have contributed to the success of marriages that you have observed.

_____

_____

_____

Basic Scriptures

The following verses give important insights for a successful marriage:

1.

> Ephesians 4:2 states: Be humble and gentle. Be patient with each other, making allowance for each other's faults because of your love. (TLB)

a. From the list below, check the actions you feel would apply to being "humble and gentle."

____ To admit error in deed or attitude when wrong

____ To wait for the other person to make amends first

____ To look for ways to help others

____ To expect what is due one's self

____ To consider timing before making requests

b. What do you think is implied in "making allowance for each other's faults"?

_____

_____

_____

c. The following are all important. However, as you consider the challenge to "be patient with each other," check the action(s) below that you find most difficult to do.

_____ To accede to the request of another with no adverse comment

_____ To take time to think before responding

_____ To not insist on having your own way

_____ To not get upset when things don't go as you had planned

Why is this difficult for you?

_____

_____

_____

2.

Philippians 2:3-4 states: Do nothing out of selfish ambition or vain conceit, but in humility consider others

better than yourselves. Each of you should look not only
to your own interests, but also to the interests of others.

a. Verse 3 says to count others better than ourselves.
Does this mean you have no rights? _____
What does it say to you?

_____

_____

b. When you marry, how will you work out verse
4—not looking out for your own things or interests, but also the interests and things of your
spouse?

_____

_____

_____

c. How do you think "do nothing out of selfish
ambition or vain conceit" applies to marriage
partners?

_____

_____

_____

Memorize and/or write out on a card Ephesians 4:2
or Philippians 2:3-4 and put it on your desk, mirror in
the bathroom, or above the kitchen sink—a place

where you can think about what it means and work on putting it into practice *now*.

Simple Guidelines

1. The Bible is full of wise counsel about being considerate. After each of the following verses, indicate the principle(s) of consideration you see in them.

> Husbands, love your wives and do not be harsh with them. (Colossians 3:19)

_____

_____

_____

> Love is patient, love is kind. It does not envy, it does not boast, it is not proud. (1 Corinthians 13:4)

_____

_____

> Husbands, in the same way be considerate as you live with your wives, and treat them with respect as the weaker partner and as heirs with you of the gracious gift of life, so that nothing will hinder your prayers. (1 Peter 3:7)

_____

_____

> The husband should fulfill his marital duty to his wife, and

likewise the wife to her husband. The wife's body does not belong to her alone but also to her husband. In the same way, the husband's body does not belong to him alone but also to his wife. Do not deprive each other except by mutual consent and for a time, so that you may devote yourselves to prayer. Then come together again so that Satan will not tempt you because of your lack of self-control. (1 Corinthians 7:3-5)

_____

_____

Let us not become conceited, provoking and envying each other. (Galatians 5:26)

_____

_____

Be devoted to one another in brotherly love. Honor one another above yourselves. (Romans 12:10)

_____

_____

2. The observance of good manners and common courtesies do not belong just to dating or courtship days but are equally important in marriage. How would you appraise yourself presently in the areas listed below?

a. Personal appearance. (What you see affects love!)

   (1) Grooming_____

   (2) Dress _____

(3) Weight_____

(4) Hair _____

b. Courtesy. (If you want to be treated like a king, treat her like a queen and vice versa.)

_____

_____

c. Etiquette.

_____

_____

d. Thoughtfulness. (Do you give expressions of love and appreciation to family and friends?)

_____

_____

Application

There may be several areas that have come to mind during this study in which you recognize that you are not being adequately considerate of others.

Which do you feel needs working on most?

_____

_____

Work out some way to check up on this, so that a

week from now you can see how you are doing. You may ask someone to check up on you, jot it down on a calendar, or write yourself a note, but do *something* to make sure you will not let it slip by.

Summary

One unappreciated wife said, "Maybe when I'm a hundred years old I'll get used to having everything I do taken for granted. As it is, life becomes pretty hard when you don't hear a word of thanks for your efforts. Sometimes I feel like copying the woman who served her menfolk cattle fodder one day for dinner after waiting twenty years for a word of praise. 'I've never heard aught to make me think you'd know the difference,' she said when they declared she must be crazy."

Thoughtful consideration for one another is an essential ingredient that each partner must put into the making of a happy marriage.

Success in this area is not automatic but has to be continually worked at so as to become a natural response. Husbands and wives have the responsibility to give proof of their high regard for each other by giving careful attention to the details of courtesy. If this is not done, the tendency will be to grow careless and offend those with whom life is lived most intimately.

It is a true axiom that says, "You are going to be what you are now becoming." If you are practicing consideration of others now (especially your family members), it will be natural to treat your mate the same way when you marry.

Recommended Reading

Rainey, Dennis. *Building Your Mate's Self-Esteem*. Nashville: Thomas Nelson, 1986.

MALE & FEMALE—

7

COMPLEMENTARY

*I*n spite of all that is known about the shortcomings of human beings and the problems in marriage, it doesn't seem to have affected the attraction of a man and a woman for each other and their desire to marry and live happily ever after. That this arrangement has been going on for centuries would indicate that it is in God's creative blueprint and in man's best interest. He made them from the beginning, male and female, and designed that they should become one, a coupling of two distinct designs (Matthew 19:4 and Ephesians 5:31).

God chose to create two sexes with the purpose that they should complement and *complete* each other—not *compete* with each other. He never intended that our differences would divide us or bring conflict but that we should appreciate those unique qualities. Both come with special standard equipment—different strengths and weaknesses, resources and needs. Each is given unique gifts to bring balance, breadth, and vitality to a relationship. Neither sex is independent of the other; rather, each is interdependent according to 1 Corinthians 11:11-12: "In the Lord, however, woman is not independent of man, nor is man independent of woman. For as woman came from man, so also man is born of woman. But everything comes from God." Each sex has equal dignity and is of unique worth to God. The stamp of God's image is on each one. There is no thought of one being superior and the other inferior.

Even in our society that is constantly rethinking the roles of men and women, the basic characteristics and built-in sexual differences between men and women have never changed. However, husbands and wives need to work out a system of roles and job assignments that will best utilize their individual gifts and build their own marriage relationship. These responsibilities have to be reevaluated and adjusted from time to time as circumstances and needs change.

Basic Roles

A few roles in life are determined by one's sex. Genesis, "the book of beginnings," records the origin of man and gives many of these primary roles.

From each of the following Scriptures list the role given and check the gender to which it applies.

> So God created man in his own image, in the image of
> God he created him; male and female he created them.
> (Genesis 1:27)

God blessed them and said to them, "Be fruitful and increase in number; fill the earth and subdue it. Rule over the fish of the sea and the birds of the air and over every living creature that moves on the ground." (Genesis 1:28)

The Lord God took the man and put him in the Garden of Eden to work it and take care of it. (Genesis 2:15)

The Lord God said, "It is not good for the man to be alone. I will make a helper suitable for him." . . . Then the Lord God made a woman from the rib he had taken out of the man, and he brought her to the man. (Genesis 2:18, 22)

For this reason a man will leave his father and mother and be united to his wife, and they will become one flesh. (Genesis 2:24)

Adam lay with his wife Eve, and she became pregnant and gave birth to Cain. She said, "With the help of the Lord I have brought forth a man." (Genesis 4:1)

Role

                                                 Male Female

1. Genesis 1:27: _____ ☐ ☐

2. Genesis 1:28: _____ ☐ ☐

3. Genesis 2:15: _____ ☐ ☐

4. Genesis 2:18, 22: _____ ☐ ☐

5. Genesis 2:24: _____ ☐ ☐

6. Genesis 4:1: _____ ☐ ☐

Scriptural Interpretation of Roles

Western culture implies that marriage is a unity created by romantic love and common interests. The Scriptures reveal that marriage is a unity created by God. A man and a woman, each having a distinct personality, background, and experiences, commit themselves to each other in marriage and become one in God's eyes. The common interests, background, education, and other things may have attracted them to each other; but it is the committal to their unity before God and man that will cause them to want to blend the "two into one."

In a Christian marriage, the partners look to God to learn how to best combine their differences and form a new identity. Since the Bible was given in part to instruct man in daily living, it contains a vast amount of truth about marriage and how to successfully maintain this all-important relationship.

1. Read Ephesians 5:21-33:

   21Submit to one another out of reverence for Christ.

   22Wives, submit to your husbands as to the Lord. 23For the husband is the head of the wife as Christ is the head of the church, his body, of which he is the Savior. 24Now as the church submits to Christ, so also wives should submit to their husbands in everything.

   25Husbands, love your wives, just as Christ loved the church and gave himself up for her 26to make her holy, cleansing her by the washing with water through the word, [27] and to present her to himself as a radiant church, without stain or wrinkle or any other blemish, but holy and blameless. [28] In this same way, husbands ought to love their wives as their own bodies. He who loves his wife loves himself. [29] After all, no one ever hated his own body, but he feeds and cares for it, just as Christ does the church— [30] for we are members of his body. [31] "For this reason a man will leave his father and mother and be united to his wife, and the two will become one flesh." [32] This is a profound mystery—but I am talking about Christ and the church. [33] However, each one of you also must love his wife as he loves himself, and the wife must respect her husband.

Now answer the following questions about this passage:

a. According to verse 21, what attitude honors Christ?

_____

b. By observing and following the example given in these verses, a husband and wife can know how they are to relate to each other. What does verse 25 say concerning the responsibility of a husband to his wife?

_____

_____

c. What are the responsibilities of being the head of a wife, a group of people, or an organization?

_____

_____

_____

d. You can better understand *how* husbands are to love their wives as you see *how* Christ loved the church. From the passage, list the characteristics of Christ's love for the church. Then compile a list showing the husband's responsibility in loving his wife, using the same passage.

Christ, Head of the Church	*Husband, Head of the Wife*
_____	_____
_____	_____
_____	_____
_____	_____
_____	_____
_____	_____

e. What do verses 22-24 say to wives?

_____

_____

_____

f. Read the statements below and check those that you believe to be accurate.

_____ The husband has been appointed head of his wife and family, and by following her husband's leadership, a wife is being obedient to Christ.

_____ A husband must possess strong leadership qualities and abilities or his wife is not expected to consider him head of their family.

_____ The relationship between Christ and his bride, the church, illustrates the relationship that should exist between husband and wife.

_____ A wife may retain the right to choose the areas in which she will be subject to her husband's leadership.

g. Using personal pronouns, put verse 33 in your own words.

_____

_____

_____

2. Look at 1 Peter 3:1-7:

[1]Wives, in the same way be submissive to your husbands so that, if any of them do not believe the word, they may be won over without words by the behavior of their wives, [2]when they see the purity and reverence of your

lives. ³Your beauty should not come from outward adornment, such as braided hair and the wearing of gold jewelry and fine clothes. ⁴Instead, it should be that of your inner self, the unfading beauty of a gentle and quiet spirit, which is of great worth in God's sight. ⁵For this is the way the holy women of the past who put their hope in God used to make themselves beautiful. They were submissive to their own husbands, ⁶like Sarah, who obeyed Abraham and called him her master. You are her daughters if you do what is right and do not give way to fear.

⁷Husbands, in the same way be considerate as you live with your wives, and treat them with respect as the weaker partner and as heirs with you of the gracious gift of life, so that nothing will hinder your prayers.

a. According to verses 1-2, what result can be expected when a wife lives in right relationship to her husband?

_____

_____

b. Do you agree with the following statements relating to verses 3-6? Check those you feel are correct.

_____ A wife is not to be concerned with how she looks.

_____ A wife's inner beauty is more important to God than her outer beauty.

_____ It was her inner qualities of a gentle and

quiet spirit that prompted Sarah to follow Abraham's leadership.

c. Read the admonition to husbands in verse 7 and answer the following questions:

(1) *How* is a husband to live with his wife?

_____

_____

(2) *Why* should a husband know and understand his wife?

_____

_____

(3) *What* do a husband and wife share equally?

_____

_____

(4) *What* interferes with a husband's prayer life?

_____

_____

Order of Responsibility and Its Results

1. God's order of responsibility in families is clearly spelled out in 1 Corinthians 11:3.

   Now I want you to realize that the head of every man is

Christ, and the head of the woman is man, and the head of Christ is God.

When each one fulfills his function properly, there will be harmony in daily living as God intends. What is the order given?

_____

_____

_____

2. **Ephesians 6:1 gives the relationship of the children in the divine order.**

   Children, obey your parents in the Lord, for this is right.

   To whom are children responsible?

   _____

3. *Humbling oneself is an act of the will.* Note in Philippians 2:5-11 how Jesus Christ willingly put himself under God's authority in order to secure man's redemption.

   [5]Your attitude should be the same as that of Christ Jesus:
   [6]Who, being in very nature God, did not consider equality with God something to be grasped, [7]but made himself nothing, taking the very nature of a servant, being made in human likeness.
   [8]And being found in appearance as a man, he hum-

bled himself and became obedient to death—even death on a cross!

⁹Therefore God exalted him to the highest place and gave him the name that is above every name, ¹⁰that at the name of Jesus every knee should bow, in heaven and on earth and under the earth, ¹¹and every tongue confess that Jesus Christ is Lord, to the glory of God the Father.

a. According to verse 6, what was Christ's position originally?

_____

b. According to verses 7-8, what did he choose to do?

_____

c. According to verses 9-11, how did God honor his obedience?

_____

4. According to 1 Peter 5:6, cited below, what will be the result of choosing to humble yourself?

Humble yourselves, therefore, under God's mighty hand, that he may lift you up in due time.

_____

5. Proverbs 31:28-31 records the praise given to a wife by her family:

²⁸Her children arise and call her blessed; her husband also, and he praises her:

²⁹"Many women do noble things, but you surpass them all."

³⁰Charm is deceptive, and beauty is fleeting; but a woman who fears the Lord is to be praised.

³¹Give her the reward she has earned, and let her works bring her praise at the city gate.

Give a short summary of their remarks.

_____

_____

6. **In Genesis 18:17-19 God makes some remarks about Abraham:**

¹⁷Then the Lord said, "Shall I hide from Abraham what I am about to do? ¹⁸Abraham will surely become a great and powerful nation, and all nations on earth will be blessed through him. ¹⁹For I have chosen him, so that he will direct his children and his household after him to keep the way of the Lord by doing what is right and just, so that the Lord will bring about for Abraham what he has promised him."

What was to be the outcome of this man's faithfulness?

_____

_____

7. Will it be difficult for you to humble yourself and take your proper place in God's order? Why?

_____

_____

Task Assignments

Some tasks must be assigned in each marriage so that daily life can run smoothly. These need not be thought of as being "feminine" or "masculine" but rather should be done by the partner best equipped to do the job. The responsibility may be exchanged from time to time as circumstances change.

1. According to Titus 2:5 who will generally be responsible for keeping the home?

> Be self-controlled and pure . . . be busy at home . . . be kind, and . . . be subject to [your] husbands, so that no one will malign the word of God.

_____

2. To whom does 1 Timothy 5:8 give the responsibility for seeing that the family is provided for?

> If anyone does not provide for his relatives, and especially for his immediate family, he has denied the faith and is worse than an unbeliever.

_____

3. List some specific task assignments in your family and the person who is responsible for them, i.e., finances, dishes, grocery shopping. Some may be shared assignments. (If you are not presently living with your parents, perhaps you can ask a couple you are acquainted with to tell you how they handle these areas.)

Task   *Person*

_____   _____

_____   _____

_____   _____

_____   _____

4. What could cause these tasks to be changed in the future?

_____

_____

Application

1. As you think through what you have learned about God's plan for roles in marriage, what do you see as your major need in preparation for your marriage?

_____

_____

2. What did the order of responsibility look like in
   your family as you grew up?

Like this?	*or this?*	*Or this?*
Wife	Children	God-Christ
Husband	Husband-Wife	Husband
Children	Christ-God	Wife
Christ-God		Children

Circle the one which was most like yours.

3. Which order do you want in your own marriage?

_____

Summary

Today traditional roles in marriage are being chal-
lenged. Some rightly so! It is necessary to understand
and apply scriptural principles when you marry so that
you will not be confused by the prevailing ideas of society, which may change tomorrow.

For maximum success and oneness, a couple must
share a strong commitment to God's purpose and to
the development of each other to be all that God
intended. True equality in a marriage is achieved when
a husband and wife come to understand, appreciate,
and honor each other's different gifts, responsibilities,
and roles.

Recommended Reading

Crabb, Larry. *Men and Women*. Grand Rapids: Zondervan, 1991.

*I*n one American city 900 wives were asked, "Why did you marry? What did you want most—financial security, sexual fulfillment, companionship, motherhood?" The most common answer was companionship—partnership. In any working and successful partnership each member brings several things to the venture. First, a strong and unwavering commitment to and appreciation of the other partner and to the purposes and objectives of the partnership. Second, each brings a set of unique gifts—a particular way of life, habits, values, attitudes, and abilities—that they contribute to the common goal.

A partnership team enables more to be accomplished than if each one worked separately. A synergistic relationship is a joint action in which the total effect is greater than the sum of their efforts when acting independently. For example, if one horse can pull 1,000 pounds and another one 1,000 pounds, hitching them together enables them to pull, not 2,000 pounds, but 3,000 pounds. Their joint effort accomplishes more.

So a strong partnership allows each one to bring his and her unique characteristics and perspective to the relationship, making the marriage richer and the possibilities greater. "Therefore what God has joined together, let man not separate" (Mark 10:9).

From courtship days "till death us do part," marriage partners must guard against that which could come between them.

Whenever anything, or anyone, poses a threat to "oneness," no matter how *good* it may seem, it is contrary to God's *best* for the marriage and must be evaluated and placed in its proper perspective in the husband and wife relationship.

In this lesson you will discover the importance of partnership at every stage of the life cycle of marriage.

Forming the Partnership

In order to establish the beginnings of partnership, it is helpful to consider the courtship and engagement stage, which is the first step toward establishing a relationship of growing oneness.

1. To the following list, add other things you feel should be a part of the engagement period.

   a. Learning to understand and relate to each other

   b. Exploring attitudes and values toward life

c. Planning details of the wedding _____

d. _____

e. _____

f. _____

g. _____

h. _____

2. The Scriptures give guidelines for the kind of relationship a couple considering marriage should have. What guidelines do you see in these passages?

> Do not be yoked together with unbelievers. For what do righteousness and wickedness have in common? Or what fellowship can light have with darkness? What harmony is there between Christ and Belial? What does a believer have in common with an unbeliever? (2 Corinthians 6:14-15)

_____

_____

> Do two walk together unless they have agreed to do so? (Amos 3:3)

_____

_____

> It is God's will that you should be sanctified: that you should avoid sexual immorality; that each of you should learn to control his own body in a way that is holy and

honorable, not in passionate lust like the heathen, who
do not know God. (I Thessalonians 4:3-5)

_____

_____

3. **Genesis 29:16-20 records Jacob's love for Rachel.**

Now Laban had two daughters; the name of the older
was Leah, and the name of the younger was Rachel. Leah
had weak eyes, but Rachel was lovely in form, and
beautiful. Jacob was in love with Rachel and said, "I'll work
for you seven years in return for your younger daughter
Rachel." Laban said, "It's better that I give her to you than
to some other man. Stay here with me." So Jacob served
seven years to get Rachel, but they seemed like only a
few days to him because of his love for her.

**Write down the evidences of love you observe in
these verses.**

_____

_____

_____

4. **What do you think is a primary area of partnership
that should be worked on during your courtship
and engagement period?**

_____

_____

Partnership before Parenthood

Marriage begins with two people, and years later, when the children are gone, it ends the same way—with just the two of them! The early months and years of marriage are vitally important as these two establish a new family system distinct from their family background. The arrival of children will add a new dimension to this relationship, but when these children later leave for homes of their own, the couple should be able to continue in unabated partnership.

1. Listed below are some of the major adjustments a couple faces in early years of marriage. Explain why you feel these are necessary for the growth of a marriage.

   a. Adjusting to the realities of marriage (which can be disillusioning after the euphoria of courtship and engagement!)

   _____

   _____

   _____

   _____

   b. Adjusting to the emotional separation from parents and family while taking on a new role of husband or wife

_____

_____

_____

_____

c. Adjusting to faults and weaknesses of a spouse
   that may have been overlooked or ignored during
   courtship when everything was idealized

_____

_____

_____

_____

d. Adjusting to knowledge that building a healthy
   marriage requires time and effort

_____

_____

_____

_____

2. A family is the basic unit of society. Why do you
   feel this is true?

_____

_____

_____

3. **The relationship that exists between Christ and the church is given in Ephesians 5:21-33 to show husbands and wives how to happily relate to one another.**

> [21]Submit to one another out of reverence for Christ.
>
> [22]Wives, submit to your husbands as to the Lord.
>
> [23]For the husband is the head of the wife as Christ is the head of the church, his body, of which he is the Savior. [24]Now as the church submits to Christ, so also wives should submit to their husbands in everything.
>
> [25]Husbands, love your wives, just as Christ loved the church and gave himself up for her [26]to make her holy, cleansing her by the washing with water through the word, [27]and to present her to himself as a radiant church, without stain or wrinkle or any other blemish, but holy and blameless. [28]In this same way, husbands ought to love their wives as their own bodies. He who loves his wife loves himself. [29]After all, no one ever hated his own body, but he feeds and cares for it, just as Christ does the church— [30]for we are members of his body. [31]"For this reason a man will leave his father and mother and be united to his wife, and the two will become one flesh."
>
> [32]This is a profound mystery—but I am talking about Christ and the church.
>
> [33]However, each one of you also must love his wife as he loves himself, and the wife must respect her husband.

Many principles can be drawn from these verses that will help to develop a gratifying partnership. Complete the list given below:

a. Verse 21: _____

_____

b. Verses 22-24: A husband is to give loving leadership and protection to his wife.

_____

c. Verse 25: _____

_____

d. Verses 26-27: A husband should desire to help his wife develop her full potential as a loved person.

_____

e. Verses 28-30: _____

_____

f. Verse 31: A husband and wife should be more to each other than to anyone else in the world.

g. Verse 33: _____

_____

4. What do you think might be one of your adjustment needs early on in your marriage?

_____

_____

Partnership and the Family

Marriage is permanent! Child rearing is only temporary. A person is not going to do much good in rearing children if he doesn't have the right relationship with his partner.

1. What are some ways a husband and wife can maintain their priority of commitment to each other when children come along?

   _____

   _____

   _____

2. Why should parents present a "united front" to their children?

   _____

   _____

   _____

3. What are some dangers for parents who overinvest in their children and underinvest in their marriage?

   _____

   _____

   _____

4. How would this affect *the children?*

_____

_____

5. What is your impression of your parents' partnership during your growing-up years?

_____

_____

6. What lesson can you learn from their relationship?

_____

_____

Partnership in the Middle Years

1. There are more divorces after twenty years of marriage than at any other time except during the first three years. What do you think contributes to the failure of partnership at this stage?

a. _____

b. _____

c. _____

2. According to Song of Solomon 8:7, cited below, how enduring should love be?

Many waters cannot quench love; rivers cannot wash it

away. If one were to give all the wealth of his house for love, it would be utterly scorned.

_____

_____

3. How can couples help each other prepare for the "empty-nest" stage?

   a. Husband can help wife by . . .

   _____

   _____

   b. Wife can help husband by . . .

   _____

   _____

4. According to the following verses, what are some of the opportunities for enjoyment during the "empty-nest" years?

   Children's children are a crown to the aged, and parents are the pride of their children. (Proverbs 17:6)

   _____

   _____

   Enjoy life with your wife, whom you love, all the days of this meaningless life that God has given you under the sun—all your meaningless days. For this is your lot in

life and in your toilsome labor under the sun.
(Ecclesiastes 9:9)

_____

_____

Brothers, I do not consider myself yet to have taken hold
of it. But one thing I do: Forgetting what is behind and
straining toward what is ahead, I press on toward the
goal to win the prize for which God has called me
heavenward in Christ Jesus. (Philippians 3:13-14)

_____

_____

5. As you examine your parents' relationship to one
   another, what area of partnership do you see that
   needs strengthening for them to meet the needs of
   middle-years crisis?

   _____

   _____

   _____

Summary

One young couple met in language school on the mission field. After a long friendship, love for each other
began to emerge and they decided to marry. Their marriage preparation included lengthy discussions on the

meaning and implications of partnership and a recognition and development of each other's innate abilities and spiritual gifts. During years of serving in several countries, and in spite of heavy responsibilities, their cooperative partnership enabled each of them to finish their graduate studies without taking away from their marriage and family priorities. So their partnership supported them while they both persistently developed their individual giftedness that now prepares them for larger service.

Partnership is more important than parenthood. How one treats and loves his marriage partner will determine what he will do with his family.

Recommended Reading

Harley, Willard. *His Needs, Her Needs*. Old Tappan, N.J.: Fleming H. Revell, 1986.

PATTERN FOR PARENTHOOD

9

*W*hen God wants a great work done in the world or a great wrong righted, he goes about it in a very unusual way. He doesn't stir up his earthquakes or send forth his thunderbolts. Instead, he has a helpless baby born, perhaps in a simple home and of some obscure mother. And then God puts the idea into the parents hearts, and they put it into the baby's mind. And then God waits.

Although child rearing will impose new responsibilities and pressures on your marriage, the Bible provides clear instructions to help you do the job. It can be the most rewarding, challenging, and enjoyable experience of a lifetime.

Remember that a husband and wife who have a mutually satisfying and growing relationship themselves already possess one important requirement for successful parenthood.

Points to Ponder

Do you think the following statements are true or false? Circle your answer, then give a brief reason for your choice.

1. **T F** One dare not sacrifice his (her) marriage partner for his (her) children.

   _____

   _____

2. **T F** The most potent influence on a child's future marriage is his (her) mother and father's relationship.

   _____

   _____

3. **T F** Because of his many responsibilities, a husband should delegate most of the training of their children to his wife.

   _____

   _____

4. **T F** The Word of God—"thus saith the Lord," should be the authoritative base upon which decisions regarding family living are made.

   _____

   _____

5. **T F** Children should be allowed to decide for
themselves if they want religious training.

_____

_____

Birth Control in Christian Marriages

Birth control is not a basic moral issue. The Bible gives
no clear or definite word for or against it. When the
Scriptures do not speak clearly and positively on a specific subject, it must then be decided on the basis of
scriptural *principles*. These must be honestly applied by
each one with a desire to discover and fulfill God's will
for the individual family.

What guidelines and principles concerning family
planning do you see in the following passages:

1. God blessed them and said to them, "Be fruitful and
    increase in number; fill the earth and subdue it." (Genesis
    1:28)

    _____

    _____

2. Sons are a heritage from the Lord, children a reward
    from him. Like arrows in the hands of a warrior are sons
    born in one's youth. Blessed is the man whose quiver is
    full of them. They will not be put to shame when they
    contend with their enemies in the gate. (Psalm 127:3-5)

_____

_____

3. If anyone does not provide for his relatives, and especially for his immediate family, he has denied the faith and is worse than an unbeliever. (1 Timothy 5:8)

_____

_____

4. If any of you lacks wisdom, he should ask God, who gives generously to all without finding fault, and it will be given to him. (James 1:5)

_____

_____

5. Husbands, in the same way be considerate as you live with your wives, and treat them with respect as the weaker partner and as heirs with you of the gracious gift of life, so that nothing will hinder your prayers. (1 Peter 3:7)

_____

_____

If birth control is used, a couple must find agreement in attitude and purpose, resulting in a shared conclusion, and select a method satisfying to both parties.

Preparing for Parenthood

Cocreating a child is a short-term biological process! Molding the character of that child takes long years of thoughtful teaching and training. One specialist in the field of human behavior said, "It probably takes more endurance, more patience, and more healthy emotion to rear a happy human being than it does to be an atomic physicist or a politician or a psychiatrist."

Preparation for child rearing requires more than a vague hope that everything will work out all right. As in all other areas of life, you must learn to accomplish right goals by an exercise of your *will*, not by emotions. Emotions can and do enter in, but emotions can be misleading. Successful parenting requires determination, preparation, planning, prayer—and hard work!

Here are some basic guidelines:

1. Review the chain of command that God has established for the family as given in the following verses.

   Now I want you to realize that the head of every man is Christ, and the head of the woman is man, and the head of Christ is God. (1 Corinthians 11:3)

   Children, obey your parents in the Lord, for this is right. (Ephesians 6:1)

2. List what you feel is involved in fulfilling Deuteronomy 6:6-7.

These commandments that I give you today are to be upon your hearts. Impress them on your children. Talk about them when you sit at home and when you walk along the road, when you lie down and when you get up.

_____

_____

3. It has been said that parents too often "major" on "minors" when it comes to training children.

a. List several character traits that you feel are necessary to develop in a child's personality. (One is listed for you.)

(1) <u>Obedience</u>

(2) _____

(3) _____

(4) _____

(5) _____

(6) _____

(7) _____

b. What are some areas of lesser importance that you feel can be overemphasized by parents?

(1) *Overconcern with clothes children wear*

(2) _____

(3) _____

(4) _____

Developing Character

Along with winning a child to Christ and teaching him the Word of God and how to pray, there are several necessary elements of character building. Children must be taught obedience without question and without argument. They must be taught how to work and to develop regular habits for happiness and usefulness, such as courtesy, manners, forgiveness, and the art of living peaceably with others.

From birth to "re-birth in Christ," your child's character foundation is built upon the relationships and examples he observes in his home.

If you as a parent follow God's teaching on character development, you can lead your child in the way of truth.

1. What does God want in his people?

> Children, obey your parents in everything, for this pleases the Lord. (Colossians 3:20)

> Do nothing out of selfish ambition or vain conceit, but in humility consider others better than yourselves. Each of you should look not only to your own interests, but also to the interests of others. (Philippians 2:3-4)

> Jesus replied: "Love the Lord your God with all your heart and with all your soul and with all your mind." (Matthew 22:37)

> In everything I did, I showed you that by this kind of hard work we must help the weak, remembering the words

the Lord Jesus himself said: "It is more blessed to give than to receive." (Acts 20:35)

Therefore each of you must put off falsehood and speak truthfully to his neighbor, for we are all members of one body. (Ephesians 4:25)

It is God's will that you should be sanctified: that you should avoid sexual immorality; that each of you should learn to control his own body in a way that is holy and honorable, not in passionate lust like the heathen, who do not know God; and that in this matter no one should wrong his brother or take advantage of him. The Lord will punish men for all such sins, as we have already told you and warned you. For God did not call us to be impure, but to live a holy life. (1 Thessalonians 4:3-7)

For we are taking pains to do what is right, not only in the eyes of the Lord but also in the eyes of men. (2 Corinthians 8:21)

And without faith it is impossible to please God, because anyone who comes to him must believe that he exists and that he rewards those who earnestly seek him. (Hebrews 11:6)

The Lord detests lying lips, but he delights in men who are truthful. (Proverbs 12:22)

Dear friends, let us love one another, for love comes from God. Everyone who loves has been born of God and knows God. (1 John 4:7)

If you love me, you will obey what I command. (John 14:15)

Match references with characteristics listed below:

a.	Obedience to God	_f._	Colossians 3:20
b.	Integrity	___	Philippians 2:3-4
c.	Truthfulness	___	Matthew 22:37
d.	Faith in God	___	Acts 20:35
e.	Purity (holiness)	___	Ephesians 4:25
f.	Obedience to parents	___	1 Thessalonians 4:3-7
g.	Honesty	___	2 Corinthians 8:21
h.	Love for God	___	Hebrews 11:6
i.	Love for others	___	Proverbs 12:22
j.	Humility	___	1 John 4:7
k.	Generosity	___	John 14:15

2. When you have a question concerning situations and choices not explicitly dealt with in the Bible, you can receive guidance by applying the following scriptural principles. Indicate what these are.

"Everything is permissible for me"—but not everything is beneficial. "Everything is permissible for me"—but I will not be mastered by anything. (1 Corinthians 6:12)

_____

_____

Therefore, if what I eat causes my brother to fall into sin, I will never eat meat again, so that I will not cause him to fall. (1 Corinthians 8:13)

_____

_____

So whether you eat or drink or whatever you do, do it all for the glory of God. (1 Corinthians 10:31)

_____

_____

So I strive always to keep my conscience clear before God and man. (Acts 24:16)

_____

_____

3. Family worship offers an ideal setting for further development of character. The scriptural admonition to parents is to represent God to their children and to present their children to God.

   As a family gathers together to worship in his presence, there is no one set pattern that should be followed. Remember, "The shorter the child, the shorter the devotions."

   a. From the following list of possible activities for family worship, check those your family tried as you were growing up.

   ____ Bible reading

   ____ Singing

   ____ Dramatization of Bible stories

____ Scripture memorization

____ Praying

____ Reading of Christian books and biographies

____ Playing records or tapes

____ Other

b. Do you think you will do anything different as you rear your children? If so, what?

_____

_____

Application

One psychiatrist noted, "Eighty percent of the problem patients that have come to me, come because manners were never taught them as children. As adults, they made mistakes and were rejected. They couldn't play the game of life because they didn't know the rules."

Are you concerned about how you will be able to build the right kind of character traits into your children? Ephesians 6:4 instructs fathers to "bring [children] up in the discipline and instruction of the Lord."

Obviously these godly characteristics must be a part of your own life before you can develop them in your children.

As a result of what you have learned in this lesson,

do you recognize a specific area of your character that needs strengthening?

What is it?

_____

What can you do about it?

_____

_____

_____

What will you do about it?

_____

_____

_____

Recommended Reading

Campbell, Ross. *How to Really Love Your Child*. Wheaton, Ill.: Victor Books, 1977.

CHILD

TRAINING

A father said to me, "Well, I'll tell you what I do. I let my children decide what they want to do. I give them a choice. If they want to go to church—fine. If they don't—fine."

I said, "That's interesting, and I imagine that makes you feel very modern. You consider yourself very generous in giving them so much freedom. The truth is you don't think as much of your children as you would a tomato plant. Have you ever grown tomatoes? Then you know that when a plant gets to a certain size, you put a stick down next to it and tie the vine up to the stick. Otherwise, your vines will be a mess all over the ground. You mean to tell me your little child is not as important to you as a tomato plant? You refuse to put any supports around him to give direction to his growth?"

The challenging tasks of rearing children will occupy many years of married life for most couples. Partners can grow together on a new and different level as they share the responsibilities and joys of bringing their children to maturity.

The goal and prayer of Christian parents is to guide their children so that they will increase "in wisdom and stature, and in favor with God and men" (Luke 2:52).

Train by Example

Telling is not *teaching! Listening* is not *learning!*

Parents teach more by *example* than by *precept* because children tend to *imitate* what they *see* rather than *do* what they *hear* if there is a conflict between the two.

In Galatians 6:7 the Bible cautions that "whatever a man sows, that he will also reap." To a great degree you will reproduce your own life in your children. If a child is given good instruction while at the same time a bad example is set for him, confusion will result. Therefore, if your child is to *be* the right kind of person, you must be sure that your life will be an example of what you teach.

1. Consult a dictionary and write a short definition of the word *train* as it applies to rearing children.

_____

2. Read Genesis 18:19, cited below, and note God's instructions to Abraham. Then consider the following statements and circle *T* for true and *F* for false.

For I have chosen him, so that he will direct his children and his household after him to keep the way of the Lord by doing what is right and just, so that the Lord will bring about for Abraham what he has promised him.

T F Abraham was to *suggest* to his family members that they follow the Lord.

T F Abraham was an example of right living to his household.

T F God left the decision to Abraham as to what he was to do.

T F God wanted to fulfill his promise to Abraham. This would be determined by Abraham's obedience.

3. In writing to the church at Philippi, what did the apostle Paul say would be the result of following his example?

Whatever you have learned or received or heard from me, or seen in me—put it into practice. And the God of peace will be with you. (Philippians 4:9)

_____

4. What are some of the things Timothy observed about Paul's life as recorded in 2 Timothy 3:10-11?

You, however, know all about my teaching, my way of life, my purpose, faith, patience, love, endurance, persecutions, sufferings—what kinds of things happened to me

in Antioch, Iconium and Lystra, the persecutions I
endured. Yet the Lord rescued me from all of them.

_____

_____

5. According to 2 Timothy 1:5, who served as examples to Timothy when he was a child?

I have been reminded of your sincere faith, which first
lived in your grandmother Lois and in your mother
Eunice and, I am persuaded, now lives in you also.

_____

_____

6. According to 2 Timothy 3:15, what was one means
of instruction for Timothy?

From infancy you have known the holy Scriptures, which
are able to make you wise for salvation through faith in
Christ Jesus.

_____

_____

7. Paul reminded Timothy, in 1 Timothy 4:12, cited
below, that he had a responsibility to set an example for others to follow. List below the areas of example given in this passage. Note beside each a specific
way parents can be an example to their children in
that area.

Don't let anyone look down on you because you are young, but set an example for the believers in speech, in life, in love, in faith and in purity.

_____

_____

_____

_____

_____

8. Who has been the person (persons) you have most often looked to as an example to follow?

_____

Train by Instruction

An important responsibility of parents is to interpret life to their children. If possible, information and principles should be taught when rules are given. Rules tell a child *what* to do, but it is needful to help him develop his own reasoning capacity by teaching him *why*.

1. Deuteronomy 6:4-7, cited below, carefully instructs parents in their responsibility toward their children. As you consider these verses, complete the following sentences.

   [4]Hear, O Israel: The Lord our God, the Lord is one. [5]Love

the Lord your God with all your heart and with all your soul and with all your strength. ⁶These commandments that I give you today are to be upon your hearts. ⁷Impress them on your children. Talk about them when you sit at home and when you walk along the road, when you lie down and when you get up.

a. As parents, my mate and I are to be wholehearted in our own response to _____

b. The Word of God is to be in our _____

c. This is not an option but a _____

d. We should _____ them on our children.

e. We should teach our children the Word when we

_____ and _____ , and when we

_____ and _____ .

2. Proverbs 22:6 reads: "Train a child in the way he should go, and when he is old he will not turn from it." The Amplified Bible says it better: "Train up a child in the way he should go [and *in keeping with his individual gift or bent*], and when he is old he will not depart from it" (italics mine).

   In other words, each child has his individual gift or bent, his own unique way. The greatest challenge of a parent is to discover the natural aptitude of each child and train them in that way so when they are grown, they will not be a failure. Each child is different—in temperament, ability, and potential. Any parent with more than one child knows this well.

Rather than compare one child with another or rear children as our parents did us, we must cooperate with God's creative plan for each child by wisely cultivating each one's special features and gifts.

Did you think your parents understood this principle?

__Yes __No

If yes, describe one way they practiced this in your growing up years.

_____

_____

3. Luke 2:52 records of Jesus Christ that he grew mentally, physically, spiritually, and socially. Each of the following verses relates to one of these four areas. Give the key thought of the passage, and check the heading, or headings, under which it fits. The first one is answered for you.

> Then little children were brought to Jesus for him to place his hands on them and pray for them. But the disciples rebuked those who brought them. Jesus said, "Let the little children come to me, and do not hinder them, for the kingdom of heaven belongs to such as these." (Matthew 19:13-14)

> Let the wise listen and add to their learning, and let the discerning get guidance. (Proverbs 1:5)

Apply your heart to instruction and your ears to words of knowledge. (Proverbs 23:12)

But grow in the grace and knowledge of our Lord and Savior Jesus Christ. To him be glory both now and forever! Amen. (2 Peter 3:18)

The woman gave birth to a boy and named him Samson. He grew and the Lord blessed him. (Judges 13:24)

And the boy Samuel continued to grow in stature and in favor with the Lord and with men. (1 Samuel 2:26)

Passage	*Key thought:*	Mental	Physical	Spiritual	Social
Matthew 19-13-14	Little children can know Jesus	□	□	□	□
Proverbs 1:5	_____	□	□	□	□
Proverbs 23:12	_____	□	□	□	□
2 Peter 3:18	_____	□	□	□	□
Judges 13:24	_____	□	□	□	□
1 Samuel 2:26	_____	□	□	□	□

Train by Love and Discipline

Love and discipline are the foundation of training a child. Love is essential from infancy through the growing years. It would be difficult for a child to become a happy, emotionally secure person without generous amounts of love! Without discipline you will not be able to teach your child to be a respectful, competent, and responsible adult. There will be no greater proof of your love than correctly applied admonition and/or discipline as it reveals your willingness to risk personal rejection (at least for a time) for the welfare of your child.

1. Read 1 Samuel 3:12-13:

> At that time I will carry out against Eli everything I spoke against his family—from beginning to end. For I told him that I would judge his family forever because of the sin he knew about; his sons made themselves contemptible, and he failed to restrain them.

Why was Eli held accountable for the wrongdoing of his sons?

2. Note the subject of discipline in Hebrews 12:5-11:

> And you have forgotten that word of encouragement that addresses you as sons: "My son, do not make light of the Lord's discipline, and do not lose heart when he rebukes you, because the Lord disciplines those he loves,

and he punishes everyone he accepts as a son." Endure hardship as discipline; God is treating you as sons. For what son is not disciplined by his father? If you are not disciplined (and everyone undergoes discipline), then you are illegitimate children and not true sons. Moreover, we have all had human fathers who disciplined us and we respected them for it. How much more should we submit to the Father of our spirits and live! Our fathers disciplined us for a little while as they thought best; but God disciplines us for our good, that we may share in his holiness. No discipline seems pleasant at the time, but painful. Later on, however, it produces a harvest of righteousness and peace for those who have been trained by it.

Put a check before the following statements that you feel are accurate.

____ The Lord never chastens anyone.

____ The chastening of the Lord is directly related to his love.

____ Disciplining is for the good of the one disciplined.

____ Disciplining is pleasurable for all concerned.

____ The purpose of administering discipline is to produce a right quality of living.

3. Proverbs 3:11-12 gives similar insight concerning discipline:

My son, do not despise the Lord's discipline and do not resent his rebuke, because the Lord disciplines those he loves, as a father the son he delights in.

What should discipline reveal about the parent's relationship to his child?

_____

_____

4. **What principle of discipline is given in Ecclesiastes 8:11?**

When the sentence for a crime is not quickly carried out, the hearts of the people are filled with schemes to do wrong.

_____

5. **Ephesians 6:4, cited below, gives guidelines for parents seeking to mold the character of their children.**

Fathers, do not exasperate your children; instead, bring them up in the training and instruction of the Lord.

a. **What does this verse say a father is to _do?_**

_____

b. **What is a father to _avoid_ doing?**

_____

_____

c. List three things a father could do which would "provoke his children to anger." (You might get some ideas from your own childhood!)

_____

_____

_____

6. The proverbs of Solomon were written that men may "know wisdom and instruction" and "understand words of insight" (Proverbs 1:2). What do you think each the following passages is saying about discipline?

> He who spares the rod hates his son, but he who loves him is careful to discipline him. (Proverbs 13:24)

_____

_____

> Discipline your son, for in that there is hope; do not be a willing party to his death. (Proverbs 19:18)

_____

_____

> Even a child is known by his actions, by whether his conduct is pure and right. (Proverbs 20:11)

_____

_____

The rod of correction imparts wisdom, but a child left to himself disgraces his mother. (Proverbs 29:15)

_____

_____

Discipline your son, and he will give you peace; he will bring delight to your soul. (Proverbs 29:17)

_____

_____

7. **As you read the following verses, think about your relationship with children that may be close to you.**

Love is patient, love is kind. It does not envy, it does not boast, it is not proud. It is not rude, it is not self-seeking, it is not easily angered, it keeps no record of wrongs. Love does not delight in evil but rejoices with the truth. It always protects, always trusts, always hopes, always perseveres. . . . When I was a child, I talked like a child, I thought like a child, I reasoned like a child. When I became a man, I put childish ways behind me. (1 Corinthians 13:4-7, 11)

a. **Do you think you exhibit the kind of love to them that this passage describes?**

____Yes ____No

b. **Do your expectations of the children you know fit their ages?**

____Yes ____No

c. Do children seem to enjoy their relationship with you?

____Yes ____No

There are four basic principles a prospective parent must remember: (1) Every parent is responsible for each child he brings into the world. (2) A parent must create an atmosphere for a child to enable him to learn maturity, responsibility, and godliness. (3) The parent is to his child what God is to the parent. (4) The parent is responsible for a child until the child is old enough to be responsible for himself.

A child should understand that his parents are themselves under God's authority and are accountable to him. Parents make mistakes and children know it! If parents err in disciplining him in anger, wrong judgment, or application, they should confess their fault to the child and ask for his forgiveness. He will learn to do this, too . . . both with them and with God!

After doing this lesson, you can better understand the importance of your parents' applying God's principles of training as they reared you. You will profit from your own experience (good or bad) when your own children come along.

Recommended Reading

Swindoll, Charles. *The Strong Family.* Portland, Oreg.: Multnomah Press, 1991.

ATMOSPHERE

11

OF THE HOME

*T*here is a difference between a house and a home!

A house is a building in which people live. A home is a place dear to one because of personal relationships, feelings of comfort and security, or warmth and fellowship. It is not only a place of personal attachment but a refuge from the demands of life.

A happy home does not depend upon material comforts for satisfaction as much as it does upon the atmosphere that is created by the family itself.

Most Christian parents have an earnest desire to see their children grow up to be successful Christian persons. They give many years of their lives to their children, investing time, prayer, thought, energy, money, and love. Godly values are communicated in an atmosphere of family love and togetherness. Fifteen hundred school children were asked the question, "What makes a happy family?" The most frequent answer was, "Doing things together." What counts most is not so much of what we do *for* each other as what we do *with* each other.

These shared fun activities and togetherness provide an atmosphere of unity and a bonding that holds a family even in tough times. This climate of closeness lasts even after the children are grown and the family is no longer physically together. They still want to return to the family setting, its memories and traditions. Home is remembered and cherished, not for the rules and regulations that existed, but for the relationships that were developed and enjoyed. In fact, if the atmosphere that existed in a home is positive and pleasant, then the teaching provided will have a stronger impact. Children are much more inclined to follow the teaching of happy people.

The Family as a Unit

A family is the total of what its members are individually, plus their interrelationships one with another. The family is the basic unit of society.

1. What fact concerning families do you see in these verses:

> So Noah went forth, and his sons and his wife and his sons' wives with him. And every beast, every creeping thing, and every bird, everything that moves upon the earth, went forth by *families* out of the ark. (Genesis 8:18-19, RSV, emphasis added)

_____

_____

2. The account of a census taken by Moses and Aaron is given in Numbers 1:17-19.

> Moses and Aaron took these men whose names had been given, and they called the whole community together on the first day of the second month. The people indicated their ancestry by their clans and families, and the men twenty years old or more were listed by name, one by one, as the Lord commanded Moses. And so he counted them in the Desert of Sinai.

How was the congregation registered?

_____

Hindrances to Family Unity

Many forces in modern living combine to threaten the "togetherness" of family life. The home is no longer the center of recreation, education, worship, or production of goods. Thus, it is difficult to maintain common interests that involve all its members.

1. Make a simple evaluation of the time your family spent *together* in a normal week (other than at mealtime). Give the approximate amount of time for each day.

Sunday _____

Monday _____

Tuesday _____

Wednesday _____

Thursday _____

Friday _____

Saturday_____

2. Families today are very mobile! Few adults live in
   the same city as grandparents, parents, or other relatives, or have much close contact with them. How
   do you think this social change affected you as you
   grew up?

   _____

   _____

   _____

Creating the Atmosphere

> By wisdom a house is built, and by understanding it is
> established; through knowledge its rooms are filled with
> rare and beautiful treasures. (Proverbs 24:3-4)

1. Like the spokes of a wheel, the closer family members are to the Hub (Christ), the closer they are to
   each other.

a. In Joshua 24:15, what commitment did Joshua make regarding his family?

> But if serving the Lord seems undesirable to you, then choose for yourselves this day whom you will serve, whether the gods your forefathers served beyond the River, or the gods of the Amorites, in whose land you are living. But as for me and my household, we will serve the Lord.

_____

_____

b. The reality of the parents' relationship to Jesus Christ will prepare their children for faith in him. What does the following verse, 1 John 1:3, say will be the result?

> We proclaim to you what we have seen and heard, so that you also may have fellowship with us. And our fellowship is with the Father and with his Son, Jesus Christ.

_____

_____

c. What is the source of family strength according to Psalm 127:1?

> Unless the Lord builds the house, its builders labor in vain. Unless the Lord watches over the city, the watchmen stand guard in vain.

_____

_____

d. Part of chapter 9 deals with family worship.
   Describe in detail how the atmosphere in your
   parents' home affected your attitude toward family worship.

_____

_____

_____

_____

2. According to Colossians 3:12-15, cited below, what
   ten things should characterize relationships in a
   Christian family?

> Therefore, as God's chosen people, holy and dearly
> loved, clothe yourselves with compassion, kindness,
> humility, gentleness and patience. Bear with each other
> and forgive whatever grievances you may have against
> one another. Forgive as the Lord forgave you. And over
> all these virtues put on love, which binds them all
> together in perfect unity. Let the peace of Christ rule in
> your hearts, since as members of one body you were
> called to peace. And be thankful.

_____

_____

_____

_____

_____

_____

_____

_____

_____

3. Each quality listed above interacts with all the others. How would you explain the relationship between the following:

a. Forgiveness and peace

_____

_____

b. Compassion and kindness

_____

_____

c. Forbearance and patience

_____

_____

The ability to forgive and accept forgiveness graciously is a necessity for building good relationships in a family. More important than fixing blame in a disagreement is the *attitude* of the people involved.

It is difficult to say, "Forgive me" or "I forgive you" without putting any conditions on the statement!

As a practical application for this lesson, what specific steps can you take to make genuine forgiveness a day-by-day part of your life?

_____

_____

_____

_____

4. What facts concerning the atmosphere in the home do you see in the following Scriptures?

How good and pleasant it is when brothers live together in unity! (Psalm 133:1)

_____

_____

Better a meal of vegetables where there is love than a fattened calf with hatred. (Proverbs 15:17)

_____

_____

Better a dry crust with peace and quiet than a house full of feasting, with strife. (Proverbs 17:1)

_____

_____

A cheerful heart is good medicine, but a crushed spirit
dries up the bones. (Proverbs 17:22)

_____

_____

Better to live on a corner of the roof than share a house
with a quarrelsome wife. (Proverbs 25:24)

_____

_____

If a house is divided against itself, that house cannot stand.
(Mark 3:25)

_____

_____

"In your anger do not sin." Do not let the sun go down
while you are still angry. (Ephesians 4:26)

_____

_____

5. Here are three other areas to be considered as you
   analyze your present home situation and look for-
   ward to the one you will have when you marry.

   a. It is important that your home be attractively
      kept and a pleasant place to live.

   b. It is important that there be a balance between
      group spirit and individuality so that each family
      member can mature as a unique person.

c. It is important that a family *enjoy* life together.
   Family activities and home life should include a
   lot of laughter, fun, and games!

   As you reflect on your childhood days, which of
   these elements were present in your family life?
   How did this affect you as a person?

   _____

   _____

   _____

There is probably nothing more damaging to creat-
ing the right home atmosphere than negative mental
attitudes. Negative thinking not only creates its own
destructive results but it permeates our reactions to
everything else that happens. Opportunities become
obstacles. Differences become disastrous. Failures are
final. We become NO people instead of YES people. It
is always our attitude, not our aptitude, that will determine our altitude.

> The longer I live, the more I realize the impact of
> attitude on life. Attitude, to me, is more impor-
> tant than fact. It is more important than the past,
> than education, than money, than circum-
> stances, than failures, than successes, than what
> other people think or say or do. It is more impor-
> tant than appearance, giftedness, or skill. It will
> make or break a company . . . a church . . . a
> home. The remarkable thing is we have a choice

every day regarding the attitude we will embrace for that day. We cannot change our past . . . we cannot change the fact that people will act in a certain way. We cannot change the inevitable. The only thing we can do is play on the one string we have, and that is our attitude. I am convinced that life is ten percent what happens to me and ninety percent how I react to it. And so it is with you . . . we are in charge of our attitudes. (Dr. Charles Swindoll)

The Home and Hospitality

The Scriptures place much emphasis upon the value of keeping an "open house" with a glad heart.

Consider the following Scriptures, then write down anything in the passage related to hospitality.

Share with God's people who are in need. Practice hospitality. (Romans 12:13)

_____

_____

Do not forget to entertain strangers, for by so doing some people have entertained angels without knowing it. (Hebrews 13:2)

_____

_____

Dear friend, you are faithful in what you are doing for the

brothers, even though they are strangers to you. They have told the church about your love. You will do well to send them on their way in a manner worthy of God. It was for the sake of the Name that they went out, receiving no help from the pagans. We ought therefore to show hospitality to such men so that we may work together for the truth. (3 John 1:5-8)

_____

_____

After this, Jesus went out and saw a tax collector by the name of Levi sitting at his tax booth. "Follow me," Jesus said to him, and Levi got up, left everything and followed him. Then Levi held a great banquet for Jesus at his house, and a large crowd of tax collectors and others were eating with them. But the Pharisees and the teachers of the law who belonged to their sect complained to his disciples, "Why do you eat and drink with tax collectors and 'sinners'?" Jesus answered them, "It is not the healthy who need a doctor, but the sick. I have not come to call the righteous, but sinners to repentance." (Luke 5:27-32)

_____

_____

Summary

There are specific and significant times in each family that can create or destroy a good home atmosphere.

There are four such times. What we do and how we act at these times will help determine whether they become positive building blocks.

1. *Morning Wake-up:* How a day starts affects its unfolding. A pleasant beginning helps ensure a positive ending. Each day should start with the affirmation, "This is the day the Lord has made. Let us rejoice and be glad in it." Our attitude upon arising is our choice, our decision. Obviously, each one has a different temperament, different metabolism, and different sleep habits, etc., but there is never any excuse for starting the day with pouting, whining, or a selfish disregard of others. Each child and adult can control his own spirit and must learn how to do it. "It is better to have self-control than to contol an army" (Proverbs 16:32, TLB).

   "Pleasant words are a honeycomb, sweet to the soul and health to the bones. . . . A cheerful heart is good medicine" (Proverbs 16:24; 17:22).

   A child going to school or an adult to work deserves to leave home with an encouragement, a warm touch, a blessing.

2. *Re-entry:* After a long day at work a husband or wife must return to their home and to each other with pleasant expectations. Each one needs time to let down—to switch gears and to prepare for dinner. This must be an oasis, a refueling. No bad news—unless the house is on fire. No litany of today's troubles. No complaints or demands. Delay the bad

news until after dinner! For now, a warm reception and welcome. Martin Luther catches the spirit: "Let the wife make her husband glad to come home, and let him make her sorry to see him leave."

3. *Mealtime:* In most cultures throughout history, eating together has been the major activity that draws the family together. It has been the heart of family communication. Even though the family sit-down dinner is less frequent than in earlier cultures, we must work to maintain its value because of its potential for building family togetherness. Sharing a meal with others creates a closeness and solidarity and is a source not only of physical strength but also of spiritual and emotional support. The family table is a training school for teaching values, a laboratory for testing ideas, an information clearinghouse, and a symbol of family unity.

A number of graduate students at the University of Chicago, when asked where they got their major ideas in morals and religion, replied, "Through the conversation in our family at mealtime." The principles that make family mealtime successful are few: (1) Strive for an unhurried atmosphere. (2) Allow no negative conversation. (3) Encourage free discussion and humor. (4) Delay disciplinary action until later. (5) Give training in table manners.

"Better a meal of vegetables where there is love than a fattened calf with hatred" (Proverbs 15:17).

4. *Bedtime:* The end of the day is the time for reflec-

tion, thanksgiving, and recharging our batteries.
Every day provides experiences that touch us, teach
us, and test us. And those prepare us for a wiser and
richer tomorrow. Expressed gratitude to God and
other family members helps keep the sun from
going down on our anger and allowing a buildup of
complaints and resentment. For children, bedtime is
also an important teaching time. In fact, the most
teachable time in a child's day is right before they
retire for the night. This is the time for a touch, a
review, an affirmation, a prayer, and a hug.

A home must be more than a place to eat and
sleep if it is to fulfill its intended purpose! The basic
emotions—the desire to be loved, to be secure, to be
needed, and to belong—are best nurtured in the relationships of the family.

Recommended Reading

Ziglar, Zig. *Courtship after Marriage*. New York: Ballan-
tine, 1992.

MONEY & ITS POSSIBILITIES

12

$\mathcal{C}$onflict over money ranks high among the causes of trouble in marriage. A careful study shows many reasons for this. Bad management is chief among them. Also, traditional attitudes and expectations regarding who should earn and spend money contribute their share of trouble. In addition, what may appear on the surface to be financial trouble may actually be personality conflict or emotional instability. Money and conflict often go hand in hand in marriage.

Millions of Americans now live on two paychecks, with the husband and wife each working outside the home. The success of a marriage often depends on the ability to handle wisely not merely their paychecks but the demands of the jobs themselves. Each one comes to marriage with different ideas regarding money and its use. Each one brings a unique history of spending or saving habits and budget, credit, priority, and investment theories. These should all be seriously considered before marriage to produce an understanding and an agreement on the meaning and management of financial goals and assets.

Money can mean many different things to people. Money not only buys the necessities of life, but it can also symbolize a measure of success, power, social status, or emotional security. Christians who acknowledge the lordship of Christ over all of their lives, including money, must be careful to *use* money and not let it use them!

Basic Attitudes

The fundamental teaching in the Scriptures about money is that of *stewardship*. A steward is one who manages *another's* property or financial affairs that have been entrusted to his care. Since God is the original supplier of all you possess, you are accountable to him to manage your resources well.

1. According to the following Scriptures, from what source does wealth come?

> Deuteronomy 8:17-18: You may say to yourself, "My power and the strength of my hands have produced this wealth for me." But remember the Lord your God, for it is he who gives you the ability to produce wealth, and so confirms his covenant, which he swore to your forefathers, as it is today.

> I Chronicles 29:12: Wealth and honor come from

you; you are the ruler of all things. In your hands are strength and power to exalt and give strength to all.

_____

_____

2. **What do the following Scriptures say about how we should feel about all that God gives us?**

Ecclesiastes 5:19: Moreover, when God gives any man wealth and possessions, and enables him to enjoy them, to accept his lot and be happy in his work—this is a gift of God.

_____

_____

1 Timothy 6:17: Command those who are rich in this present world not to be arrogant nor to put their hope in wealth, which is so uncertain, but to put their hope in God, who richly provides us with everything for our enjoyment.

_____

_____

3. **Put Ecclesiastes 5:10 into your own words.**

Whoever loves money never has money enough; whoever loves wealth is never satisfied with his income. This too is meaningless.

_____

_____

4. **One of the strongest admonitions concerning money is found in 1 Timothy 6:6-10.**

> But godliness with contentment is great gain. For we brought nothing into the world, and we can take nothing out of it. But if we have food and clothing, we will be content with that. People who want to get rich fall into temptation and a trap and into many foolish and harmful desires that plunge men into ruin and destruction. For the love of money is a root of all kinds of evil. Some people, eager for money, have wandered from the faith and pierced themselves with many griefs.

The statement *You can't take it with you!* comes from this passage. What other truths about money do you observe here?

a. _____

b. _____

c. _____

d. _____

5. **Note the teaching of Christ concerning money in Luke 12:13-21:**

> [13] Someone in the crowd said to him, "Teacher, tell my brother to divide the inheritance with me."
>
> [14] Jesus replied, "Man, who appointed me a judge or

an arbiter between you?" ¹⁵Then he said to them, "Watch out! Be on your guard against all kinds of greed; a man's life does not consist in the abundance of his possessions."

¹⁶And he told them this parable: "The ground of a certain rich man produced a good crop. ¹⁷He thought to himself, 'What shall I do? I have no place to store my crops.'

¹⁸"Then he said, 'This is what I'll do. I will tear down my barns and build bigger ones, and there I will store all my grain and my goods. ¹⁹And I'll say to myself, "You have plenty of good things laid up for many years. Take life easy; eat, drink and be merry."'

²⁰"But God said to him, 'You fool! This very night your life will be demanded from you. Then who will get what you have prepared for yourself?'

²¹"This is how it will be with anyone who stores up things for himself but is not rich toward God."

a. In verse 15, why did Jesus caution against covetousness?

_____

b. In verse 20, why do you think God called the rich man a fool?

_____

6. Hebrews 13:5, cited below, encourages valuing God's priorities rather than man's. What warning do you see in this verse?

> Keep your lives free from the love of money and be content with what you have, because God has said, "Never will I leave you; never will I forsake you."

_____

_____

7. The following Scripture passage, Philippians 4:11-13, reveals the secret Paul had learned that enabled him to be content regardless of his financial state:

> I am not saying this because I am in need, for I have learned to be content whatever the circumstances. I know what it is to be in need, and I know what it is to have plenty. I have learned the secret of being content in any and every situation, whether well fed or hungry, whether living in plenty or in want. I can do everything through him who gives me strength.

State his secret in your own words.

_____

_____

The attitude of one's heart first toward God and then toward possessions is what is most important in God's sight. This will eliminate the ever-present danger of placing your trust in your resources rather than in God.

8. Do you feel you have acknowledged Christ as Lord of your financial life? Explain your answer:

_____

_____

Using Money Wisely

To get money is difficult, to keep it more difficult, but to spend it wisely is the most difficult of all.

Family management of money requires thoughtful effort to avoid problems. Here are some basic principles regarding earning and spending money:

1. How will most of the necessities for a family be provided according to 2 Thessalonians 3:7-12?

> For you yourselves know how you ought to follow our example. We were not idle when we were with you, nor did we eat anyone's food without paying for it. On the contrary, we worked night and day, laboring and toiling so that we would not be a burden to any of you. We did this, not because we do not have the right to such help, but in order to make ourselves a model for you to follow. For even when we were with you, we gave you this rule: "If a man will not work, he shall not eat." We hear that some among you are idle. They are not busy; they are busybodies. Such people we command and urge in the Lord Jesus Christ to settle down and earn the bread they eat.

_____

_____

2. What practical example does Proverbs 6:6-8 give for consideration?

> Go to the ant, you sluggard; consider its ways and be wise! It has no commander, no overseer or ruler, yet it stores its provisions in summer and gathers its food at harvest.

_____

_____

3. Taxes are a very real part of life today. What do the following verses teach about them?

> This is also why you pay taxes, for the authorities are God's servants, who give their full time to governing. Give everyone what you owe him: If you owe taxes, pay taxes; if revenue, then revenue; if respect, then respect; if honor, then honor. (Romans 13:6-7)

_____

_____

> After Jesus and his disciples arrived in Capernaum, the collectors of the two-drachma tax came to Peter and asked, "Doesn't your teacher pay the temple tax?" "Yes, he does," he replied. When Peter came into the house, Jesus was the first to speak. "What do you think, Simon?" he asked. "From whom do the kings of the earth collect duty and taxes—from their own sons or from others?" "From others," Peter answered. "Then the sons are exempt," Jesus said to him. "But so that we may not offend them, go to the lake and throw out your line. Take

the first fish you catch; open its mouth and you will find a four-drachma coin. Take it and give it to them for my tax and yours." (Matthew 17:24-27)

_____

_____

Then the Pharisees went out and laid plans to trap him in his words. They sent their disciples to him along with the Herodians. "Teacher," they said, "we know you are a man of integrity and that you teach the way of God in accordance with the truth. You aren't swayed by men, because you pay no attention to who they are. Tell us then, what is your opinion? Is it right to pay taxes to Caesar or not?" But Jesus, knowing their evil intent, said, "You hypocrites, why are you trying to trap me? Show me the coin used for paying the tax." They brought him a denarius, and he asked them, "Whose portrait is this? And whose inscription?" "Caesar's," they replied. Then he said to them, "Give to Caesar what is Caesar's, and to God what is God's." When they heard this, they were amazed. So they left him and went away. (Matthew 22:15-22)

_____

_____

4. **According to 1 Corinthians 4:1-2, what should the character of a Christian steward reveal?**

So then, men ought to regard us as servants of Christ and as those entrusted with the secret things of God.

Now it is required that those who have been given a trust must prove faithful.

_____

_____

5. **What does Proverbs 22:7 say is the relationship of a borrower to a lender?**

The rich rule over the poor, and the borrower is servant to the lender.

_____

6. **What do these verses teach about the financial responsibility family members should have for one another?**

Then some Pharisees and teachers of the law came to Jesus from Jerusalem and asked, "Why do your disciples break the tradition of the elders? They don't wash their hands before they eat!" Jesus replied, "And why do you break the command of God for the sake of your tradition? For God said, 'Honor your father and mother' and 'Anyone who curses his father or mother must be put to death.' But you say that if a man says to his father or mother, 'Whatever help you might otherwise have received from me is a gift devoted to God,' he is not to 'honor his father' with it. Thus you nullify the word of God for the sake of your tradition. (Matthew 15:1-6)

_____

_____

Now I am ready to visit you for the third time, and I will not be a burden to you, because what I want is not your possessions but you. After all, children should not have to save up for their parents, but parents for their children. (2 Corinthians 12:14)

_____

_____

If anyone does not provide for his relatives, and especially for his immediate family, he has denied the faith and is worse than an unbeliever. (1 Timothy 5:8)

_____

_____

7. A budget is an estimate of what a family's income and expenses will be, and anyone who wants a realistic guide for planning and spending will find it absolutely essential to prepare one. Do you have a workable plan for handling your finances?

_____

A good plan to follow is the 10-70-20 formula. This makes provision for savings and investment, living expenses, and debts all at the same time. Always lay aside 10 percent for your future estate. That's 10 percent of your net income after taxes and tithe have been paid—not a saving for some future purchase, but as an investment so you will not end your years as a burden on your family or on society.

Never allow your living expenses to exceed 70 percent. This will include home payments, medical and insurance costs, utilities, home maintenance, miscellaneous. Use 20 percent to pay debts. It is easier to pay debts than to ignore them. But you must have a plan. And that plan must provide that you pay not more than 20 percent of your net income to rid yourself of back bills. John Wesley said it well: "Make all the money you can, save all the money you can, and give all the money you can."

How to Give

The secret of living is giving. Three biblical principles make this clear. "It is more blessed to give than to receive" (Acts 20:35). "Give, and it will be given to you" (Luke 6:38). "He who sows generously will also reap generously" (2 Corinthians 9:6).

God is an economist. He entrusts larger gifts to those who use the smaller ones well. Christ's parable in Luke 12:48 teaches that we must increase our income as much as possible for our Master. To whom much is given, much is required.

God's work in the world could be increased significantly if today's Christians would give what they should now and then earn more so they could give more. To be a partner with God in his worldwide mission is the highest privilege any person can enjoy.

1. **What is the first principle of giving for Christians as stated 2 Corinthians 8:5?**

    And they did not do as we expected, but they gave themselves first to the Lord and then to us in keeping with God's will.

    _____

    _____

2. **As you read 2 Corinthians 9:6-12, note some other principles concerning giving. Add to the list given below:**

    Remember this: Whoever sows sparingly will also reap sparingly, and whoever sows generously will also reap generously. Each man should give what he has decided in his heart to give, not reluctantly or under compulsion, for God loves a cheerful giver. And God is able to make all grace abound to you, so that in all things at all times, having all that you need, you will abound in every good work. As it is written: "He has scattered abroad his gifts to the poor; his righteousness endures forever." Now he who supplies seed to the sower and bread for food will also supply and increase your store of seed and will enlarge the harvest of your righteousness. You will be made rich in every way so that you can be generous on every occasion, and through us your generosity will result in thanksgiving to God. This service that you perform is not only supplying the needs of God's people but is also overflowing in many expressions of thanks to God.

a. Giving should be a matter of personal conviction.

b. Giving should be a joy for the giver.

c. _____

d. _____

e. _____

f. _____

3. Mark 12:41-44 tells of Jesus observing a widow contributing to the temple treasury.

> Jesus sat down opposite the place where the offerings were put and watched the crowd putting their money into the temple treasury. Many rich people threw in large amounts. But a poor widow came and put in two very small copper coins, worth only a fraction of a penny. Calling his disciples to him, Jesus said, "I tell you the truth, this poor widow has put more into the treasury than all the others. They all gave out of their wealth; but she, out of her poverty, put in everything—all she had to live on."

a. Why did he praise her?

_____

_____

b. How did others contribute?

_____

_____

4. **What, according to Matthew 6:1-4, will be the result of giving with false motives?**

> "Be careful not to do your 'acts of righteousness' before men, to be seen by them. If you do, you will have no reward from your Father in heaven. So when you give to the needy, do not announce it with trumpets, as the hypocrites do in the synagogues and on the streets, to be honored by men. I tell you the truth, they have received their reward in full. But when you give to the needy, do not let your left hand know what your right hand is doing, so that your giving may be in secret. Then your Father, who sees what is done in secret, will reward you."

_____

_____

5. **To whom should you give?**

> Give generously to him and do so without a grudging heart; then because of this the Lord your God will bless you in all your work and in everything you put your hand to. There will always be poor people in the land. Therefore I command you to be openhanded toward your brothers and toward the poor and needy in your land. (Deuteronomy 15:10-11)

_____

_____

> Anyone who receives instruction in the word must share all good things with his instructor. (Galatians 6:6)

_____

_____

If we have sown spiritual seed among you, is it too much if we reap a material harvest from you? . . . In the same way, the Lord has commanded that those who preach the gospel should receive their living from the gospel. (1 Corinthians 9:11, 14)

_____

_____

If anyone has material possessions and sees his brother in need but has no pity on him, how can the love of God be in him? Dear children, let us not love with words or tongue but with actions and in truth. (1 John 3:17-18)

_____

_____

6. **Malachi 3:10 states an Old Testament view of giving with which 1 Corinthians 16:2 agrees.**

"Bring the whole tithe into the storehouse, that there may be food in my house. Test me in this," says the Lord Almighty, "and see if I will not throw open the floodgates of heaven and pour out so much blessing that you will not have room enough for it." (Malachi 3:10)

On the first day of every week, each one of you should set aside a sum of money in keeping with his income, saving it up, so that when I come no collections will have to be made. (1 Corinthians 16:2)

Check the following list as you note each statement in these verses.

_____ Giving should be planned.

_____ Giving should be done at a regular time.

_____ Giving should be proportional to income.

_____ Giving is rewarded by God.

7. What does Philippians 4:15-19 promise those who give to the Lord's work?

> Moreover, as you Philippians know, in the early days of your acquaintance with the gospel, when I set out from Macedonia, not one church shared with me in the matter of giving and receiving, except you only; for even when I was in Thessalonica, you sent me aid again and again when I was in need. Not that I am looking for a gift, but I am looking for what may be credited to your account. I have received full payment and even more; I am amply supplied, now that I have received from Epaphroditus the gifts you sent. They are a fragrant offering, an acceptable sacrifice, pleasing to God. And my God will meet all your needs according to his glorious riches in Christ Jesus.

_____

_____

8. Are you satisfied with the system you now have for channeling funds for giving?

_____

Summary

....

In a marriage whether one or both partners contribute to the family income, it is important to operate in a *"we"* relationship: *"our"* money, not *"my"* money! Each mate should have some money for personal needs and desires and not have to give an accounting for it. Money designated for your marriage enrichment should also be in the budget. This would be for any books, tapes, seminars, retreats, honeymoon weekends, or vacation getaways that would help to strengthen and improve your marriage. After discussion, agreement should be reached regarding the handling of finances, remembering that in this area, as in all others, God ultimately holds the husband responsible as head of the home.

Many conflicts about money can be avoided if marriage partners are familiar with specific areas of financial responsibility and come to a mutual decision regarding them.

If you are now engaged, in addition to the motives and actions studied in this lesson, you and your fiancée may need to reach an understanding about the areas listed below.

Put a check beside the ones you have already discussed.

____ Setting a Christ-centered living standard

____ Credit buying

____ Spending for recreation

____ Children's future education

____ Insurance plans

____ Making a will

____ Savings and investments

____ Long-term financial planning

"William's Partner"
by Philip Jerome Cleveland

It was a bright, promising day when a boy just sixteen years of age said farewell to his people and turned into the wide world to seek his fortune. As he trudged along, an aged gentleman, captain of a canal boat, recognized the boy and stepped to his side.

"Well, William, where are you going?"

"I don't know," answered the honest lad. "I must make a living for myself."

"There is no trouble about that. Just be sure you start right, and you'll get along nicely."

"But there is only one trade I know."

"And what is that, my boy?"

"Making soap and candles."

The old salt grasped the boy's shoulder as he said: "Well, let me pray with you once more and give you an old man's advice. Then I will let you go."

The two knelt and prayed. Then the captain spoke seriously. "Someone will soon be the leading soap maker in New York. It might as well be you as the next fellow. I sincerely hope it will be you. Be a good man, William; give your heart to the Carpenter of Nazareth."

The old man paused a moment and then looked deeply into the youth's solemn eyes. "Listen, William. Give the Lord all that truly belongs to him, a portion of every dollar you ever earn. Make an honest soap, give a full pound, and I am certain that the Lord will bless you. Make him your partner, William."

The lad thanked the earnest captain and turned his face toward the great city. Lonesome and far from home, he nevertheless remembered words his mother had spoken to him and the advice of the aged Christian man. He decided to seek first the kingdom of heaven and become a Christian.

The first dollar earned brought up the matter of the tenth—the Lord's share. "If the Lord will take one-tenth, I will give that."

Ten cents on every dollar was set aside for the work of the Master. He engaged in the soap business, made an honest soap, and gave a full pound. He said to his bookkeeper one day: "Enter an open account with the Lord in our business book."

"Wh-what?" stammered the bookkeeper.

"An open account with the Lord, and carry one-tenth of all our income in the ledger. It shall be his!"

William prospered, and his business doubled, then tripled; he found himself growing rich. "Give the Lord two-tenths," he ordered a few months later.

Business increased amazingly. "Give the Lord three-tenths." Soon the message was changed to four-tenths and five-tenths.

Never did a soap manufacturer have a more surprising and stunning rise to fame and popularity and fortune.

And what was the name of the boy who followed an old canal-boat captain's advice? It is known all over the world even today for fine soap—William Colgate.

Recommended Reading

Burkett, Larry. *Answers to Your Family's Financial Questions*. Wheaton, Ill.: Tyndale House, 1991.

*A*ll aspects of life are intertwined, and each must be given proper attention and effort. We all tend to become one-dimensional creatures, focusing primarily on only one aspect of life. Becoming lopsided we bump down the road—out of balance—increasing our wear and tear, our stress and distress.

You can be intellectually sharp, but a dull marriage partner—a disciplined physical specimen but a spiritual dwarf. It is God's desire that we experience life in all its fullness and become peak performers. The defining element of a peak performer is a sense of balance.

The healthy closeness of a Christ-centered marriage should extend far beyond the four walls of the home to enrich our job, our church, the community, and the world.

Your Job and Your Employer

Human labor is a blessing. It provides challenges, excitement, adventure, and rewards that nothing else does. However, according to one career consultant, about 80 percent of the population is in the wrong job. The toll of chronic job dissatisfaction on a wage earner and his family is high. Loss of self-esteem and self-respect, family tension and anxiety, anger, and a low level of frustration gnaw at the emotional and spiritual health of both parties.

Almost all satisfied workers share one thing in common. They do work that is consistent with their God-given abilities, talents and interest.

1. What principles do the following verses have in common?

> 2 Thessalonians 3:10: For even when we were with you, we gave you this rule: "If a man will not work, he shall not eat."

> 2 Thessalonians 3:12: Such people we command and urge in the Lord Jesus Christ to settle down and earn the bread they eat.

> Genesis 3:19: "By the sweat of your brow you will eat your food until you return to the ground, since from it you were taken; for dust you are and to dust you will return."

_____

_____

2. Romans 13:7 concerns one's responsibility to governing authorities. How could it be applied to your responsibility to an employer?

> Give everyone what you owe him: If you owe taxes, pay taxes; if revenue, then revenue; if respect, then respect; if honor, then honor.

_____

_____

3. Ephesians 6:5-9 gives instructions to employees and employers. Read the passage and the statements below. Then circle either *T* for true or *F* for false.

> Slaves, obey your earthly masters with respect and fear, and with sincerity of heart, just as you would obey Christ. Obey them not only to win their favor when their eye is on you, but like slaves of Christ, doing the will of God from your heart. Serve wholeheartedly, as if you were serving the Lord, not men, because you know that the Lord will reward everyone for whatever good he does, whether he is slave or free. And masters, treat your slaves in the same way. Do not threaten them, since you know that he who is both their Master and yours is in heaven, and there is no favoritism with him.

T F I am to do my work as "unto the Lord."

T F I am responsible to obey those for whom I work.

T F My objective at work is to impress my employer.

T F The attitude I maintain at work is not important.

T F God is not particularly interested in the quality of work I do.

T F As an employer, I am responsible to God for the kind of "boss" I am to my employees.

4. How can you best do your work as "unto the Lord"? List at least three conclusions from Titus 2:9-10.

> Teach slaves to be subject to their masters in everything, to try to please them, not to talk back to them, and not to steal from them, but to show that they can be fully trusted, so that in every way they will make the teaching about God our Savior attractive.

a. _____

b. _____

c. _____

5. According to 1 Corinthians 10:31, why is it important to have a wholehearted attitude toward your job?

_____

_____

_____

6. Have you identified your God-given abilities and gifts so you can prepare for the job or career that will bring you the greatest satisfaction and success?

_____ Yes _____ No

If your answer is no, you should consider a vocational/psychological test that would help you discover your natural gifts and aptitudes.

A word of caution concerning your job may be needed. A person who *neglects* his family, however successful he may be before the world, is a failure before God. Some husbands—and some wives—give their family everything, everything but themselves! Determine now not to let this happen in your marriage.

Your Church

The Christian home does not stand alone but is part of a larger family. The church is God's family of families. Although parents hold and share the prime responsibility for the spiritual nurturing of their children, they soon recognize that they need input from other sources. The local church can give this encouragement and, in so doing, undertakes *supplementing* parental instruction and training.

1. A great many church members attend worship services *only* "for the sake of the children." There are other sound reasons given in Scripture for congregating with the family of God. From the following Scriptures indicate these reasons.

   Acts 8:25: When they had testified and proclaimed the

word of the Lord, Peter and John returned to Jerusalem, preaching the gospel in many Samaritan villages.

Acts 20:28: Keep watch over yourselves and all the flock of which the Holy Spirit has made you overseers. Be shepherds of the church of God, which he bought with his own blood.

---

1 Corinthians 11:23-26: For I received from the Lord what I also passed on to you: The Lord Jesus, on the night he was betrayed, took bread, and when he had given thanks, he broke it and said, "This is my body, which is for you; do this in remembrance of me." In the same way, after supper he took the cup, saying, "This cup is the new covenant in my blood; do this, whenever you drink it, in remembrance of me." For whenever you eat this bread and drink this cup, you proclaim the Lord's death until he comes.

Ephesians 4:11-13: It was he who gave some to be apostles, some to be prophets, some to be evangelists, and some to be pastors and teachers, to prepare God's people for works of service, so that the body of Christ may be built up until we all reach unity in the faith and in the knowledge of the Son of God and become mature, attaining to the whole measure of the fullness of Christ.

Hebrews 10:24-25: And let us consider how we may spur one another on toward love and good deeds. Let us not give up meeting together, as some are in the habit of doing, but let us encourage one another—and all the more as you see the Day approaching.

_____

2. What definition does your dictionary give for *worship* as it relates to God?

_____

_____

3. List some of the activities you enter into in the performance of *worship* at your church.

_____

_____

_____

_____

4. Acts 2:42 records the four most basic activities of the early church as they met together.

They devoted themselves to the apostles' teaching and to the fellowship, to the breaking of bread and to prayer.

Using your own words, describe what they did.

_____

_____

_____

_____

5. **What should you expect from the leaders of your church? Fill in the blanks.**

Jeremiah 3:15: "Shepherds" (spiritual leaders) are to lead those in their care with _____ and _____.

1 Peter 5:2-4: Shepherds are to tend (guard, guide, care for) those in their charge, not _____ but _____. In all that they do they are to be _____ to the flock.

6. **According to Hebrews 13:7, what responsibility does God give to those in the church concerning leaders?**

Remember your leaders, who spoke the word of God to you. Consider the outcome of their way of life and imitate their faith.

a. **The general congregation:**

_____

_____

b. **The leaders:**

_____

_____

_____

Although the family and the local church should have a strong relationship to one another, care should be exercised lest involvement become so heavy there is little time for the family itself to be together!

Personal Ministry

1. Matthew 5:16 indicates an important aspect of your daily life.

   In the same way, let your light shine before men, that they may see your good deeds and praise your Father in heaven.

   a. What do you think this verse is saying?

   _____

   _____

   _____

   b. Explain how you think this could be accomplished.

   _____

   _____

   _____

2. What do the following passages say about a Christian's responsibilities to those around him?

Mark 16:15: He said to them, "Go into all the world and preach the good news to all creation."

_____

_____

2 Corinthians 5:18-20: All this is from God, who reconciled us to himself through Christ and gave us the ministry of reconciliation: that God was reconciling the world to himself in Christ, not counting men's sins against them. And he has committed to us the message of reconciliation. We are therefore Christ's ambassadors, as though God were making his appeal through us. We implore you on Christ's behalf: Be reconciled to God.

_____

_____

Colossians 1:28-29: We proclaim him, admonishing and teaching everyone with all wisdom, so that we may present everyone perfect in Christ. To this end I labor, struggling with all his energy, which so powerfully works in me.

_____

_____

Matthew 28:18-20: Then Jesus came to them and said, "All authority in heaven and on earth has been given to me. Therefore go and make disciples of all nations, baptizing them in the name of the Father and of the Son and of the Holy Spirit, and teaching them to obey everything I have commanded you. And surely I am with you always, to the very end of the age."

_____

_____

2 Timothy 2:2: And the things you have heard me say in
the presence of many witnesses entrust to reliable men
who will also be qualified to teach others.

_____

_____

3. The admonition to "make disciples" requires knowing what is involved in *being* a disciple. Use your dictionary to define the word *disciple*.

_____

_____

4. Discover what the Scriptures teach about discipleship. Record your findings below.

   Luke 9:23: Then he said to them all: "If anyone would
   come after me, he must deny himself and take up his
   cross daily and follow me."

   _____

   _____

   John 8:31: To the Jews who had believed him, Jesus said,
   "If you hold to my teaching, you are really my disciples."

   _____

   _____

   John 13:34-35: A new command I give you: Love one

another. As I have loved you, so you must love one another. By this all men will know that you are my disciples, if you love one another.

_____

_____

John 15:8: This is to my Father's glory, that you bear much fruit, showing yourselves to be my disciples.

_____

_____

Luke 6:46: Why do you call me, "Lord, Lord," and do not do what I say?

_____

_____

As a result of this study on discipleship, what has God said to you?

_____

_____

What will you do in response?

_____

_____

Be sure your personal ministry to others is in perspective to your time with your family.

Stewardship of Time

A common problem facing the modern family is the pressure of time!

The question of how individual family members can meet the demands for involvement in the community and still maintain good communications with one another is not easily answered.

1. A biblical injunction regarding the use of your time is found in Ephesians 5:15-17.

> Be very careful, then, how you live—not as unwise but as wise, making the most of every opportunity, because the days are evil. Therefore do not be foolish, but understand what the Lord's will is.

Complete the list below relating to this verse.

a. I must be careful how I act.
_____

b. I must exercise wisdom in my life.
_____

c. _____

d. _____

e. _____

2. James states that a man's life is short and uncertain (James 4:14). In light of this knowledge, write Psalm 90:12 in your own words as a prayer request to God.

Teach us to number our days aright, that we may gain a heart of wisdom.

_____

_____

_____

Your life is continually undergoing change, making it necessary to keep close watch on maintaining your priority relationships.

The purpose of these lessons has been to provide a means by which you can better understand the marriage relationship from God's perspective.

A *perfect* marriage does not exist. But if and when you marry, as you and your mate apply God's Word to your lives, God will enable you to experience all that he intended when two become one.

Recommended Reading

Waitley, Denis. *Seeds of Greatness.* Old Tappan, N.J.: Fleming H. Revell, 1983.

Other Books by J. Allan Petersen

The Marriage Affair
For Families Only
For Men Only
For Women Only
Conquering Family Stress
The Myth of the Greener Grass
Hi-Fidelity Marriage
Two Become One (a Bible Study)

Self-help booklets
Making Marriage Work
You Are Really Somebody

Family Affair tapes
These two-volume, eight-cassette albums contain Dr. Petersen's complete and well-known Family Affair seminar series. Presented in hundreds of cities with thousands of cooperating churches, this dynamic series provides practical and effective insights for many aspects of marriage and family living.

Other Living Books Best-sellers

ANSWERS by Josh McDowell and Don Stewart. In a question-and-answer format, the authors tackle sixty-five of the most-asked questions about the Bible, God, Jesus Christ, miracles, other religions, and Creation. 07-0021-X

THE BELOVED STRANGER by Grace Livingston Hill. Graham came into her life at a desperate time, then vanished. But Sherrill could not forget the handsome stranger who captured her heart. 07-0303-0

BUILDING YOUR SELF-IMAGE by Josh McDowell and Don Stewart. Here are practical answers to help you overcome your fears, anxieties, and lack of self-confidence. Learn how God's higher image of who you are can take root in your heart and mind. 07-1395-8

THE CHILD WITHIN by Mari Hanes. The author shares insights she gained from God's Word during her own pregnancy, identifying areas of stress, offering concrete data about the birth process, and pointing to God's promises to lead those who are with young. 07-0219-0

COME BEFORE WINTER AND SHARE MY HOPE by Charles R. Swindoll. A collection of brief vignettes offering hope and the assurance that adversity and despair are temporary setbacks we can overcome! 07-0477-0

DR. DOBSON ANSWERS YOUR QUESTIONS by Dr. James Dobson. In this convenient reference book, renowned author Dr. James Dobson addresses heartfelt concerns on many topics, including marital relationships, infant care, child discipline, home management, and others. 07-0580-7

THE EFFECTIVE FATHER by Gordon MacDonald. A practical study of effective fatherhood based on biblical principles. 07-0669-2

FOR WOMEN ONLY by Evelyn R. and J. Allan Petersen. This balanced, entertaining, and diversified treatment covers all the aspects of womanhood. 07-0897-0

HOW TO BE HAPPY THOUGH MARRIED by Tim LaHaye. A valuable resource that tells how to develop physical , mental, and spiritual harmony in marriage. 07-1499-7

Other Living Books Best-sellers

JOHN, SON OF THUNDER by Ellen Gunderson Traylor. In this saga of adventure, romance, and discovery, travel with John—the disciple whom Jesus loved—down desert paths, through the courts of the Holy City, and to the foot of the cross as he leaves his luxury as a privileged son of Israel for the bitter hardship of his exile on Patmos. 07-1903-4

LIFE IS TREMENDOUS! by Charlie "Tremendous" Jones. Believing that enthusiasm makes the difference, Jones shows how anyone can be happy, involved, relevant, productive, healthy, and secure in the midst of a high-pressure, commercialized society. 07-2184-5

MORE THAN A CARPENTER by Josh McDowell. A hard-hitting book for people who are skeptical about Jesus' deity, his resurrection, and his claim on their lives. 07-4552-3

QUICK TO LISTEN, SLOW TO SPEAK by Robert E. Fisher. Families are shown how to express love to one another by developing better listening skills, finding ways to disagree without arguing, and using constructive criticism. 07-5111-6

REASONS by Josh McDowell and Don Stewart. In a convenient question-and-answer format, the authors address many of the commonly asked questions about the Bible and evolution. 07-5287-2

RUTH, A LOVE STORY by Ellen Gunderson Traylor. Though the pain of separation and poverty would come upon her, Ruth was to become part of the very fulfillment of prophecy—and find true love as well. A biblical novel. 07-5809-9

THE SECRET OF LOVING by Josh McDowell. McDowell explores the values and qualities that will help both the single and married reader to be the right person for someone else. 07-5845-5

THE STORY FROM THE BOOK. From Adam to Armageddon, this book captures the full sweep of the Bible's content in abridged, chronological form. Based on *The Book*, the best-selling, popular edition of *The Living Bible*. 07-6677-6

Other Living Books Best-sellers

THE STRONG-WILLED CHILD by Dr. James Dobson. With practical solutions and humorous anecdotes, Dobson shows how to discipline an assertive child without breaking his spirit. Parents will learn to overcome feelings of defeat or frustration by setting boundaries and taking action. 07-5924-9

SUCCESS! THE GLENN BLAND METHOD by Glenn Bland. The author shows how to set goals and make plans that really work. His ingredients for success include spiritual, financial, educational, and recreational balances. 07-6689-X

THROUGH GATES OF SPLENDOR by Elisabeth Elliot. This unforgettable story of five men who braved the Auca Indians has become one of the most famous missionary books of all time. 07-7151-6

WHAT WIVES WISH THEIR HUSBANDS KNEW ABOUT WOMEN by James Dobson. The best-selling author of *Dare to Discipline* and *The Strong-Willed Child* brings us this vital book that speaks to the unique emotional needs and aspirations of today's woman. An immensely practical, interesting guide. 07-7896-0

WHY YOU ACT THE WAY YOU DO by Tim LaHaye. Discover how your temperament affects your work, emotions, spiritual life, and relationships, and learn how to make improvements. 07-8212-7

You can find Tyndale books at fine bookstores everywhere. If you are unable to find these titles at your local bookstore, you may write for ordering information to:

**Tyndale House Publishers
Tyndale Family Products Dept.
Box 448
Wheaton, IL 60189**